PAYERS

A F
CTION T
ZE

C. Wddy

Va® Judson Press

Prayers: From Adoration to Zeal
© 1993
Judson Press, Valley Forge, PA 19482-0851

Library of Congress Cataloging-in-Publication Data
Gaddy, C. Welton.
        Prayers: from adoration to zeal/C. Welton Gaddy
            p.   cm.
        ISBN 0-8170-1190-0
        1. Prayers. I. Title
        BV 245.G343 1993   -9254
        242'.8--dc20   CIP

Printed in   Printed in the U.S.A.

                94 95 96 97 98 99 00 01   9 8 7 6 5

To

Hyran Barefoot
William E. Callahan
Charles D. Taylor

In memoriam
Willis H. Kimzey, Jr.

Professors at Union University who,
by their lectures,
introduced me to the God who cares
for all of life and enjoys interaction
with all creation; by their lives,
nurtured within me an honest Christian faith;
and by their friendship,
enriched my personhood and
filled me with enduring gratitude.

Contents

Introduction

Prayers are for God. Only! Prayers are a person's praises, protests, questions, confessions, petitions, intercessions, promises, and commitments honestly, openly, searchingly, and humbly offered to God. Prayers are intended to begin a conversation with God or to respond to a revelation from God. Prayers can continue a dialogue with God.

Some prayers come easily, others painfully. Prayers can be the spontaneous results of external circumstances or internal feelings, as well as the studied statements of words born of disciplined devotion.

Prayers are sometimes responses of faith. At other times, they are requests for faith. Prayers may focus on issues no larger than the parameters of one individual's personality or encompass subjects much bigger—concerns as broad as the world. Prayers can be formed boldly amid heaves of great laughter or sighed hesitantly between heavy sobs accompanied by tears.

Honesty is the highest priority in prayer. In fact, dishonesty disqualifies words as prayers—even the most pious-sounding, seemingly sincerely offered communiqués. God is not deceived. God will not abide subterfuge, half-truths, cover-ups, and pseudohumility. An honest denial of God by an atheist is more akin to true prayer than routine words about God captured in clichés and paraded before God as substitutes for gut-wrenching confessions and heart-stopping cries for help. Only honest communication to God qualifies as prayer.

Both public prayer and private prayer are important. In public prayer, one person speaks to God in front of, and often on behalf of, many other persons. Such prayer facilitates a focus on God, to whom the prayer is offered, and sets before God concerns with which numerous people identify and sense involvement. The language of public prayer requires words and phrases inclusive of all who hear it.

More than once, the preeminent preacher George Buttrick told me of his conviction that a pastoral prayer offered to God as an act of congregational worship should receive as much time and attention as the sermon to be delivered in that service. Though I have not always strictly adhered to my friend's advice with hour-for-hour precision, I have conscientiously labored at getting ready to pray to God in public, especially in public worship.

Praying in public has been and continues to be an integral dimension of my ministry. Like many other people, I have offered prayers in an almost endless variety of settings—at the opening sessions of conventions devoid of any observable religious associations but determined at least to nod at God; standing in waiting rooms outside the surgical units of hospitals surrounded by anxious relatives of a patient; preceding a lecture in a classroom; before a microphone in the sterile chambers of a city council; at the dedication ceremonies of new buildings; at the opening of an art exhibit; beside an open grave surrounded by grieving family members and friends; behind a kneeling rail at the conclusion of a bride and groom's statement of their marriage vows; in the living room of a couple consecrating their house to God; at the lectern facing a mass of graduates about to receive academic degrees; gathered around a table at a banquet; behind the bars of a state prison as people labeled "criminals" seek the resources of faith; in the locker room of athletic teams about to compete; seated around a conference table at the beginning of a church committee meeting; behind a pulpit while serving as a leader of corporate worship.

Private prayer differs from public prayer. When a person prays one-on-One with God, what matters most are a person's honest expressions of praise, gratitude, confession of sins, guilt, requests for forgiveness and help, concerns for others, needs, and commitments. In private prayer, the pronoun "I" is not a sign of egoism but is an indication of intimate personal confession.

The substance of a public prayer can be appropriated by an individual and meaningfully offered to God as a private prayer. However, that principle cannot be reversed. A public forum is not the place for private praying.

The prayers in this volume are both public and private offerings to God. Distinguishing between the two is easy. A repetitive use of the first-person singular pronoun occurs only in prayers formed in solitude and extended as private communiqués to God. Plural pronouns dominate my public prayers.

Both public and private prayers are important. They are not identical in nature, though; neither can serve as an acceptable substitute for the other. Substance, not style, is the major concern in these prayers. Impressive words, exemplary sentence structure, and proper paragraph development in prayers have no value if the deepest issues of a person's (or a people's) heart are not placed before God in a straightforward manner. In prayers, brevity is no more a virtue than great length.

The format of a prayer matters little—whether carefully written in advance so every word can be chosen meticulously or uninhibitedly blurted out when whatever comes to mind is voiced in a strictly stream-of-consciousness manner. Obviously many of my prayers, both private and public, have been written. But my manner of prayer carries no claims of authority for anyone else. Authentic praying stems from genuine efforts at communicating with integrity. Prayers are for God. Only!

God is the sole audience for the prayers in this volume. God is addressed as "you" rather than "thou" to increase a sense of divine-human intimacy.

My efforts in prayer are accompanied by the same hesitancy and feelings of inadequacy that hound most people who seek to pray. In no sense are the prayers presented here viewed as examples to be copied. Only one model prayer exists, and its author has no peers.

So why this book? My single intent is to offer assistance. Close friends have encouraged me to publish some of my prayers, and others have asked for copies of prayers offered in diverse settings. Thus, I have decided to set in a larger context prayers best understood as the sentiments of one person trying to take seriously himself, the Christian faith, the demands of discipleship, and the preoccupations of human beings in the global community as he prayed to God.

When someone needs to pray (publicly or privately) and finds it difficult to get started, perhaps these prayers can prompt thoughts and encourage emotions that start that person's words flowing. If my prayers ever hinder a reader's prayers, they should be set aside immediately.

The printed prayers that follow are offered to God. They are arranged alphabetically as a matter of convenience for a reader who is looking for help in speaking to God about a particular concern. These prayers embrace radically diverse emotions and deal with a great variety of subjects. However, the topics most apparent in these prayers make up the terrain traversed by all Christian pilgrims.

An unprinted prayer accompanies each of the printed prayers that follow. As I submit these very personal offerings to God for readership by others, I set before God a sincere request that my words will be read in such a manner that all who see them are helped in the framing of their own prayers to God. Finally, I pray that the prayers in this book will bring glory to God.

Adoration

Majestic God:

We speak to you with unqualified, unrestrained adoration. We do so much want you to hear our words of exaltation.

Really, God, we are stunned. Seldom do we encounter moments or events that elicit from us one word after another of praise and adoration.

We do well verbalizing the dynamics of waiting for such phenomena. We have done more than our share of waiting. We know, at least in part, about articulating joy. But just to stand or sit or kneel before One who is so holy that nothing other than adoration seems appropriate, that is different—very different.

Enable us to reach into the depths of our beings and find those words and phrases that best acclaim your greatness.

The beauty of the earth proclaims the glory of your creation.

We adore you, O God.

Authentic ministries of the church dramatically demonstrate the
breadth of your compassion.

We adore you, O God.

The faith of Christian disciples heralds the gift of your
Incarnation.

We adore you, O God.

A fellowship of concerned believers
declares as well as portrays the reconciling power of
your redemption.

We adore you, O God.

Wherever we look, however we look, we see evidences of your care—

the glory of a sunset,

the majesty of mountains,

the cry of a newborn baby,

a reunion of longtime friends,

the roar of an ocean.

We adore you, O God.

We are overwhelmed by your goodness. Nowhere at any time have we ever seen a love like that which comes to us . . .

from a cross on a hill shaped like a skull . . .

around a Communion table from which we are served . . .

when we have failed miserably and find ourselves drenched

in guilt . . .
in an experience of grinding grief.
    We adore you, O God.
We recognize you as the Creator, the Savior, the Forgiver, the Reconciler. We know you are as active in our lives as you are in our world.
    We adore you, O God.
    We adore you, O God,
        with our words, thoughts, and actions;
        with our lips, hands, and feet,
        with our hymns, prayers, and offerings.
So marvelous is your grace, so wonderful your love, so beautiful your Son, that we feel the need for all creation to unite in adoration—to function as a cosmic chorus adoring you. We certainly will do our part.
    We adore you, O God.
And we express our adoration in the name of your Son. Amen.

Advent

God of our waiting, Author of our hoping:
    Our anticipation increases as Advent begins. Once again we set ourselves to waiting. That's not easy, God. It seems like we spend most of our lives leaning forward, looking ahead, talking about what will be, waiting. In fact, sometimes we really grow weary of always being on the verge of everything and rarely ever in the middle of anything. At least anything very significant or special.
    Teach us patience, God. During Advent instruct us in waiting. Enlighten us regarding confidence born of fulfillment so that we can know the difference between
        hoping and hallucinating,
        waiting and escaping,
        praying and dreaming,
        anticipating and fantasizing.
O come, O come, Emmanuel.
    We are watering down smoldering coals scattered around a
        powder keg in the Middle East.
    We are hurting with brothers and sisters seeking freedom in
        numerous Third World nations.

We are readjusting charts and refiguring schedules in a
frantic effort to stabilize our economy.
We are searching for ways to facilitate peaceful
revolutions in Central America.
And all of that does not even address the hurts, hospitalizations,
business concerns, and family issues of our individual lives.
O come, O come, Emmanuel.
Anxious, we need assurance.
Lonely, we long for your presence.
Shrouded in darkness, we look for light.
Surrounded by silence, we want to hear a word of hope.
Besieged by alienation, we seek reconciliation and the gift
of salvation.
O come, O come, Emmanuel.
We are more accustomed to missiles than to mangers.
We spend more time plotting defense strategies and devising
plans of attack than launching peace initiatives.
We need the Christ.
O come, O come, Emmanuel.
In Warsaw and Moscow.
In Bogotá and San Salvador.
In London and Paris.
In Beijing and Washington.
In our lives.
Anticipation builds as Advent begins. And we wait once more. No
particular virtue or special grace marks our waiting. We wait because
we have to. But because of the fulfillment that inevitably follows the
promise of Advent, we wait now also because we want to.
We are ready
to receive the divine gift,
to shout for joy at a birth,
to celebrate unbroken fellowship,
to delight in redemption,
to herald Christmas Day.
We know we must wait. The time is not yet. So we wait. While
waiting, though, we continue to pray.
O come, O come, Emmanuel. Amen.

Ambivalence

O God of paradox and understanding:

Ambivalence is our constant companion. We live lives of ambivalence—

as nomads and permanent residents,
in doubt and in belief,
on mountaintops and in valleys,
with shouts of hallelujah and with pleas for help,
as saints and as sinners,
with despair and with hope.

We live with ambivalence. And, God, it wears us out. We find ourselves

weak when we want to be strong,
wanting to laugh but needing to cry,
knowing our social responsibility but seeking to find rest
in radical individuality.

At moments we want to emulate those persons who seem always to have an answer for every question and to declare it with certainty, but we don't know how to square this attitude with an integrity that confesses finiteness and acknowledges mystery. Sometimes we think we would like to lose ourselves in worship. But it is in worship that we find ourselves. When we run to you to get away from everything, invariably, while enjoying your gift of sabbath rest, we find the will and strength to head back into the fray.

Compassionate God, please deliver us from ambivalence. If that is not possible, though, or if that is not a responsible move for your people, make us fit for ambivalence. Remind us that you are with us always and in all ways, even in the midst of ambivalence.

We offer this prayer with certainty in the name of the One who was perfect paradox. Amen.

Anger

God:

I'm mad! Really, frighteningly mad. "Anger" is not the word to describe what I feel. When I am angry, I possess a modicum of reason. I get angry

at stupid statements passed off as spiritual truths,

at cancer cells that attack the bodies of good, productive people,

at government officials who use their positions for selfish gain rather than for service,

at churches that refuse to demonstrate the grace they declare,

at social systems that demean individuals in desperate need of a sense of dignity,

at self-righteous people who give goodness a bad reputation,

at suffering among innocent children,

at narrowness and closed-mindedness camouflaged as courageous conviction.

My anger leads me to positive actions. With your assistance, I can focus anger and harness its energy to work on good causes.

Right now, though, I am not angry. I am mad. I am mad at some individuals whose very names strike a burning in my thoughts. Their actions represent everything I dislike. And their attitudes are even worse. In my opinion, of course.

God, I need help. I see no way to be this mad and not sin. My irrational emotion has the potential for explosive expressions in destructive words and actions. Frankly, at moments I don't care, but I do at present. That's why I am praying now. I do not want things to get worse.

Ironically, those people I am so mad at don't even know of my feelings toward them. All of this rage within me is not affecting them in any way. But, God, it is ruining me. Realistically, I am aware that if I "go off"—explode as a walking time bomb—the result will be more suicidal than harmful to others. I will hurt myself as well as those who care for me. Those people I'm mad at will not feel any-thing at all.

Though I know I ought to give up this dangerous feeling, for some sad reason, I like it. I don't want to let go of my anger because I don't know what to do next. I readily see why "madness" is the most descriptive term for this state of mind and emotion.

Whether out of a selfish desire to experience relief and to avoid self-destruction or out of a personal commitment to moral discipline, I am asking you, O God, to help me be done with being mad. I don't think I can love those individuals yet. I can't honestly pray for them. But I do want to stop being mad at them.

Please help me God, through Jesus Christ in whom anger was a virtue, not a madness. Amen.

Art

Inspiring God, who calls us to enjoy beauty and participate in creation:

We are somewhat fickle about art. We are moved to tears while we stand in front of a canvas filled with Rembrandt's mastery of light and darkness or ponder the distortions of the present age as captured in the barely discernible figures of Picasso. But we can experience the same deep emotion when looking at the simple fingerpainted scene of a first grader or when listening to the piano recital of a teenager. We have known a profound hush of awe when studying Michelangelo's sculpture of David and a complete captivation of our attention as we gazed at "The Last Supper" by da Vinci. At the same time, we applaud crude clay figures molded by elementary school students and ceramic trinkets fired in a senior citizens' craft class. We have felt a deep sense of appreciation as members of an audience enthralled by performers in live theater. We also have realized intense gratitude while staring at bathrobe-clad shepherds and cardboard-winged angels making their way down an aisle during a local church's Christmas pageant.

We are grateful to you for all the media of art that keep us in touch with beauty, truth, reality, and faith and for artists whose works elicit from us hurt, sorrow, compassion, and joy. You enrich our lives by the divine gifts of talents, creativity, and carefully honed skills that produce spirit-nurturing art.

Giver of all good, help us discover our roles as co-creators in your world, to discern our potential as artists. Then work within us that we might sense inspiration and direction for our discoveries. Make us bold enough to take the risk of creativity. Accept the art we craft—
the texts we write,
the songs we sing,

the performances we give,
the stories we tell,
the pictures we paint, and
the models we sculpt.
Receive as artistic gifts as well
our parenting of children,
our caring for the ill,
our teaching of lessons,
our encouraging of the downhearted,
our forgiving of wrongdoers,
our befriending of the lonely, and
our gracing of the ordinary.
Hear, O God, our goal. The object of our art is not to receive others' praise for ourselves; rather, it is to offer expressions that give glory to your name and bring you pleasure.

We offer this prayer in the name of the One who has been, is, and will be both the most dominant inspiration and subject in art. Amen.

Autumn

O God of nature and all its seasons:

I had no intention of praying right now, but at this particular moment, I cannot help but reach out to you. An early-morning meeting took me away from my house in that last bit of darkness that prevails before the daily eruption of light. A slight chill in the air, indicative of the season, ensured that I was wide awake and alert. Then came the sun—a magnificent red sphere hurling hundreds of thousands of rays of light filtered through the dark green needles of pine trees set against a brilliant blue sky. And the leaves of the other trees! O God, how do you do it?

Bright green leaves that have brought shade during the summer now look like someone has indiscriminately dabbed them with varying hues of the prettiest colors in creation. Looking across a field browned by ready-to-harvest soybeans and dried cornstalks, I see a cluster of trees that stands like a big bouquet of flowers. Harmony—a harmony of striking beauty—has been formed out of diversity, a variety of reds, oranges, yellows, golds, and greens.

Sometimes during this season I get very sad. Everything of beauty in nature seems to be dying. Falling leaves foretell falling temperatures. Many of us fear the certain iciness of winter in our souls as well as in our world. We shudder at the thought.

But today I stood in the afternoon sun and felt its warmth. I sensed that I was being flooded by your love as I sat, talked, and laughed with a matchless friend. What incredible joy. What a remarkable moment. A collage of colors surrounded us—a kind of cosmic signature by which you assure us of your presence. Suddenly I realized that all winter long warmth will come from that spherical traveler through the sky—our source of light—and that the love of good friends will dispel the harshest chill. Of course, the constancy of your compassion is beyond question.

Now I know you have made provision for what we need most, not in order for us just to endure any season, but for us to live, really live in all seasons. The sun assumes its high place in the heavens every day. The life-giving experience of communion with friends is undeterred by any kind of adverse forces within or without. You have promised to be with us always.

It is autumn, O God. We behold the beautiful leaves and what promise, as well as hope, we find in close friends. It is autumn. Thanks be to you, O God.

Thanks be to you in the name of the perfect Person for all seasons. Amen.

Benediction

God of arrivals and departures, past and future:

It is time to be going. We seek not to get away from you. Rather, we request that your benediction be upon us in the form of your presence with us. But we must go—from here.

Truths need telling.

Treaties need signing.

Songs need singing.

Books need writing.

Sermons need preaching.

Hungry people need feeding.

Hurting people need comforting.

Lonely people need loving.

Ideas need implementing.

Jobs need doing.

Students need teaching.

Wars need stopping.

Communities need healing.

It is time for us to be going. Go with us, God, and stay with us that we may be singers and authors, truth tellers and lovers, thinkers and peacemakers, comforters and healers—that we may be your kind of people.

We go praying to you and, as best we can, following after you. Amen.

Bible

God of revelation:
Please accept our prayer of gratitude for your Holy Word found in the Bible.

We know of our indebtedness to numerous persons who, acting as your servants, have aided our understanding of the Bible. Thanks be to you

for our Jewish predecessors who preserved the words of Law,
Wisdom, and the Prophets, and the songs of the psalmist,

for first-century Christians who recorded on parchment what
they had heard, seen, and felt regarding the Christ,

for persons in subsequent centuries who have translated the
Hebrew and Greek texts into different languages that all
people might benefit from Scripture,

for scholars who have devoted their lives to researching
and interpreting the profound meaning of biblical materials.

We pray that the entirety of our lives will be open to the whole truth of the Bible in order for your Holy Word

to channel our emotions properly,

to still our anxieties,

to inform our lives,

to comfort our inner pain,

to strengthen the durability of our hope,

to resolve our doubts,

to nurture our faith,

to provide us peace,

to point us to redemptive forgiveness,

to speak to us good news.

Stop, please, our squabbling about the Bible. Prevent us from worshiping the Bible rather than you, the God of the Bible. Deliver us from equating our opinions about the Bible with the messages and meaning of the Bible.

Strengthen us as we seek to be good stewards of the Bible, speaking its truth in love and embodying its truth with integrity.

When we gather in fellowship so that your Word can minister to us, inspire us to disperse with commitment so that we can be ministers of your Word to others; in the name of the Word who became flesh. Amen.

Birth

God of the Nativity, Mary, and Joseph:

A child is born!

A flood of emotions sweeps over us. We do not know whether to laugh or cry, to run, dance, or scream in hilarity over the gift of new life in our midst, or to sit and ponder the awesome responsibility of receiving new life among us.

We do know we are thankful—so very thankful and appreciative! This baby embodies the goodness with which you continue to fill our lives and bring hope to our world. Thank you, God.

O God, show us how to love this little girl in such a way that as soon as she knows anything at all, she knows she is loved. Enable us to create a community in which she can grow, as did your Son, in wisdom and stature and in favor with you and with other persons.

Protect this small, whimpering bundle of physical flesh and spiritual potential. And later, guide her. Throughout her life, give her safety in the presence of dangers to her body and grace in the face of temptation. Sensitize her to constant reminders that she is your child.

Instill within her a love for you that results in her own confession of Jesus Christ as Lord and a determination to live as a "handmaid of the Lord" like her sister Mary before her.

We pray in the name of Jesus, whose redeeming life began in the form of a wiggling, gurgling, cooing, dependent-upon-others baby. Amen.

Burdens

O God:

If the burdens in our hearts were weights on our shoulders, we would not even be able to walk, much less stand up straight. We are carrying heavy loads:

> promises made in the past that are too tough to keep in the present;
>
> obligations that have piled up to form an unmanageable heap;
>
> depression that slows our pace at best and at worst makes us dysfunctional;
>
> anxieties that set us on edge, drain our energies, and leave us worn out;
>
> unconfessed sins that torment our consciences and ravage our spirits;
>
> grief that constantly lurks just beneath the surface of our emotions and regularly emerges to devour even a hint of joy;
>
> dreams that appear destined to die.

Long ago, through the ministry of Jesus, you invited us to come to you when our lives close in around us, when problems become insurmountable, when burdens bend our souls as well as our backs, and when the direction of our lives seems to point toward hell. Here we are, God. That is our condition.

Jesus promised that your yoke is easy and your burden light. Not so ours. We are ready to swap. O God, please lift our burdens so we can shoulder yours.

We ask in the name of the One who readily recognized overburdened people and invited them, and summons us, into your comforting presence. Amen.

Business Meeting

Sovereign God:

Another meeting! More business. We speak to you about time and people.

All of us know the frustrations and disappointments of too many meetings—

meetings for the sake of meeting,

meetings for the sole purpose of planning other meetings,

meetings that substitute talk for action,

meetings that waste time and energy.

None of us need another meeting like that. So as we begin to meet just now, we pray that this meeting will be different. We pray for a productive use of time and the emergence of meaningful moments in the course of this conference.

May participants be able to speak of help derived from this
meeting rather than just of meeting.

May information be acquired that can make a difference for
good in the quality of the lives of people with whom we
work.

That brings us to speak to you about people. Keep constantly before us the priority of persons.

Challenge us when our plans and conversations about
administrative charts, salary structures, personnel policies,
staff realignments, and the like are insensitive to the people
involved—persons with talents and needs.

Make us see faces and feel relationships as we ponder
conflict resolution, performance evaluations, and financial
compensation.

Prevent us from reducing individuals to numbers and
elevating institutional things over personal beings.

Sovereign God, we speak to you about time and people in the name of the One who redeems people and enables people to redeem time. Amen.

Christmas Eve

It is almost midnight on Christmas Eve. I am ready for the joyful experience of exchanging presents with family members in the morning. In fact, I still feel some of the excitement that has been associated with this special evening since childhood. But before I lie down to sleep, I need to speak with you, O God.

All the decorations around me are indicative of the season. With every blink, the Christmas tree lights seem to say, "Christmas, Christmas, Christmas." (I must remember to unplug those lights before I go to bed.) Yet, sitting here on the sofa, I see nothing in this room that bears any resemblance at all to a stable. And I'm not sure I have ever seen a real manger. I am wondering what this indicates about the prospects of your Son's coming to me.

I am not a shepherd. At no time during this season have I even donned a robe in order to play one. If I were to hear singing angels, or see them, I would not know what to do with them.

But I *do* want you to come into my world, into my life. I invite you here and now. I welcome you.

Please come here as you came to Bethlehem. I long for a recognition of your permanent presence. I need the guidance of your wisdom in all my deliberations.

Come, Lord Jesus. Be born in me. Live in my house. Abide in my life. Amen.

Church

Faithful God who delights in communities of faith:

As we begin to pray for the church, we wonder if we even need to pray for the church. After all, the church is your idea. Christ got it going. Your Spirit keeps it alive and gives it strength. Is this prayer necessary?

Surely the stirrings within our souls evidence your answer to our questions. *We* are the church. And you know we need prayer. Praying for ourselves is as essential to life as breathing. So we do pray for the church:

We give thanks for the church—
    for its support of biblical proclamation,
    for its provision of religious education,

for its call to corporate worship,
for its involvement in person-centered ministries.
Thanks, God.
We request forgiveness for the church—
for equating facilities and fellowship,
for bowing to human expectations for success rather than
conforming to Christ's expectations of faithfulness,
for shrinking back from adventure and failing to risk,
for allowing talk about grace to act as a substitute for
acting with grace,
for commending ourselves and our programs rather than
exalting you and offering salvation.
Forgive us, God.
We pray for change in the church—
when our praise is not persistent and contagious,
when our prayers are not fervent and constant,
when our ministries are not vibrant and relevant,
when our message is not pastoral and prophetic,
when our evangelism is not enthusiastic and comprehensive.
Change us, God.
We pray for the renewal of the church.
Deepen our devotion.
Give breadth to our compassion.
Awaken our dulled consciences.
Sharpen our blurred visions.
Quicken our redemptive actions.
Renew us, God.
We pray for your guidance for the church. Lead us
as we listen to people's needs and seek the best ways to
respond,
as we assess community weaknesses and attempt to provide
strength,
as we face failures and ponder the possibility of success,
as we attempt conformity to the biblical revelation amid
the diversity and controversy of public opinion.
Guide us, God.
O God of the church, enable us to be worthy examples of the
people for whom Christ died, with whom Christ continues to work,
and in whom Christ lives. Amen.

Commitment

God of promises and fulfillment:
Sometimes we would like to renegotiate this matter of commitment. It seems so total—and final.
Would you not settle for one day a week? Or one talent out of several? Or a percentage of our money rather than all of it?
Would you settle for less than our lives? Of course not. You gave everything—everything—to us. Here are our lives, O God. Amen.

Community

God of individuals and groups:
Going it alone in this world no longer makes any sense (if it ever did). In moments of clarity, we recognize our need for one another.
As we pursue a sense of commonality, though, we have only faint hopes of ever discovering community. We are overwhelmed by the reality of diversity.
Sharp distinctions and important differences pull us apart.
We look at one another with stereotypical prejudices and
try to understand one another by means of uncritical biases.
God, in the past you brought unity out of diversity. Please do it again among us. Set before us a compelling vision of our common humanity. Help us to see one another as human beings—each unique, each precious, each even holy in a strange sort of way.
Then enable us to allow your summons to cooperation and fellowship to form the basis for a community that we can never achieve on the basis of mutuality or kindred identity. Focus our attention on your invitation to togetherness that transcends individual differences and draws us into a special society.
In the name of the One who calls us to you and binds us to one another, we pray for experiences of the joy that comes from knowing meaning individually and finding fellowship in community. Amen.

Competition

God of grace:

We come into your presence as winners and losers. Like it or not, and many of us don't like it, that seems to be the way our lives get organized and labeled.

> We win or lose golf matches, tennis tournaments, and
> softball games.
> We win or lose spelling contests and scholarships.
> We win or lose new contracts, court cases, and clients.
> We win or lose elections.

Competition so dominates our natures that developing community is extremely difficult work—hard to strive for, harder still to attain.

O God, you may not understand. You never have seemed very interested in winning and losing, victories and defeats—except when love, justice, integrity, and the like were tested. You refuse to see winners and losers, for you value and love all people.

Let us learn from you, O God. Weaken our interest in categorizing people as victors or losers. Mold us into a community in which all have equal status and a place of honor. Form among us a fellowship in which every individual gives thanks for the victory of faith over despair, love over hatred, and life over death.

We pray in the name of the Christ—the ultimate winner in the eyes of some, a pitiable loser in the eyes of others, but Savior for all. Amen.

Confession

Graceful God of forgiveness:

Confession doesn't come easily for us. Thanksgiving is easy—we can talk at length about what we have received. Praise flows freely from our lips—we can speak readily of your glory and of what we have been able to do by means of your Spirit. But confession is another matter. Confession disturbs us.

We do not like the conclusion that we are sinners. Not that we have any illusions about being saints. But we try hard. We work toward worthy goals. We attempt responsible lifestyles. Surely you understand that we do not want to admit insufficiency and acknowledge our finitude.

Here is our confession, however. We need forgiveness. We are weary of carrying heavy guilt. We seek your divine pardon.

Forgive us, O God, for loudness—

    for talking when we should be listening,

    for proclaiming when we should be praying,

    for impatience about what ought to be when we need to
        accept what is,

    for relentless busyness when we should find renewing
        restfulness.

Forgive us, O God, for silence—

    for feeling love and failing to whisper it,

    for reeling with joy and not shouting "hallelujah,"

    for knowing truth and forfeiting an opportunity to teach it,

    for sensing a need to share our faith and squelching it,

        thereby blunting the sharp leadership of the Holy Spirit.

Forgive us, O God, for self-righteousness—

    for judging people rather than helping them,

    for criticizing folks rather than comforting them,

    for talking about friends in trouble rather than walking
        with them.

Honestly, God, if Jesus had told us to cast a stone at someone only if we were without sin, I am afraid that someone would have been killed by stoning. Not because we are perfect people, but because, when it comes to our own sins, we are dishonest people.

Forgive us, O God, for incompleteness—

    for not growing in Christ,

    for not expanding our knowledge of the Scriptures,

for not developing our talents,
for not deepening our relationship with the church,
for being satisfied with less than we can be,
for believing less than we know to believe,
for behaving at a level far below our capacity for
    growing,
for giving well under our potential to share.

God, our involvement in wrong seems so private. Our hatred appears self-contained. Our selfishness seems under control. Our preference for evil is disguised. So often we see our involvement in evil as understandable, even excusable. After all, we have not taken any prisoners. We have attempted no assassinations. We have cast no votes for war. We have not withheld bread from anyone whom we have known to be starving or failed to offer help to someone who is obviously hurting.

Why must you press us for full disclosure? Yes, we have manipulated people and then made them our captives. We have murdered a few folks with our words about them (though we would never even so much as point a gun at them). We have prospered apathetically while others have starved silently. We have condoned the jealousy and prejudice that are warlike on a less than global scale—factors that are devastating in both interpersonal and international relations.

O God, we see. We see more than we want to see. Please forgive us.

We can't go on and on, though. Surely that will suffice for confession. It seems like much more than enough.

Actually, we would like to hear from you now. Will you accept us? Will you forgive us?

Did we hear you say yes? Is that really your voice? Are you, the Lord of the universe, really granting us forgiveness for the wrong in our lives? Yes? Yes!

Good God, thank you. Thank you, God! You are our shepherd, our light, our salvation, our mercy seat, our crying place, our forgiving master, our rejoicing Savior, our reigning Lord.

Thank you. Thank you, God! Amen.

Controversy

God of the wilderness:

Controversy swirls around us. We can barely take care of daily chores because of a preoccupation with charges and countercharges, petitions, protests, press conferences, and rumors. Controversy stirs up mixed feelings within us.

However much we do not know, we do know our need for you and the help that comes from your divine presence.

Strengthen us so that we do not fear controversy when truth
is at stake and fundamental principles are under attack.

Enlighten us so that we can distinguish between what can be
negotiated and what should never be compromised.

Provide us with discriminating wisdom so that we can attack
issues but respect the persons involved in them.

Grant us discernment so that we can know where our rights
end and the rights of others begin.

From the example of Jesus we have learned that sometimes controversy is unavoidable. Indeed, at times it is essential and beneficial. But we hesitate to enter any controversy apart from your guidance. Specifically, we seek to emulate the spirit of our Lord in this time of crisis.

Guide us, O God. Show us how to be your kind of people in bad times as well as good, amid disagreements as well as consensus.

We pray in the name of the controversial Christ. Amen.

Crucifixion

God:

I didn't do it! I am not responsible for the crucifixion of Jesus. Never in a thousand years would I have nailed him. I love him. I believe in him. I try to follow him. I just did not do it. I don't know why this somber feeling grips me when I think of the cross. I am innocent . . . or at least I am innocent of this dastardly deed.

Sure, I have done a few things wrong. Sometimes I hedge on the truth a little, just a little. I am not dishonest. I just do not say all that could be said or respond to questions that are not asked.

I never have killed anyone with a knife or a gun. Occasionally, I do enjoy passing along a good rumor—even if it tears down somebody else. But it is just talk, you understand.

Adulterous thoughts, scandalous ideas, evil fantasies—yes, I entertain them, but usually without implementation.

I never would take your name in vain or worship an idol, though I admit my behavior does not always square with my belief, and my priorities get out of line from time to time. Maybe I do serve some lesser gods. Not many, though, and not often.

You can count on me never betraying you. I cannot stand Judas because of what he did. Of course, I do like to gripe about the church. And I will own up to saying some pretty (maybe ugly is a more appropriate word) critical things about your people.

Why, O God, do I have this terrible feeling, this awful sense of involvement with that motley crowd at Golgotha? I did not do it—I don't think. These are my wrongs. I have told you. Maybe they are worse than I first thought. But surely they are not that bad. Not bad enough to kill the Messiah. Are they?

Are they, God?

If these kinds of wrongs killed Jesus . . . if this is what the crucifixion was, and is, all about, then, O God, I need forgiveness. I need forgiveness badly.

Great God, forgive me. Please.

I come to you in the name of the Savior. Amen.

Death

God of life and death:

Thoughts of death frighten us. It is not a matter of unbelief. Honest, it's not. We believe in your all-embracing love. We have faith in the reality of uninterrupted fellowship with you. We believe.

When family members and friends die, we grieve. Without arguing the point about them being better off, we miss them and we realize that we will continue to miss them. Maybe our pain stems from selfishness. Honestly, though, it seems to be the child of love and devotion.

Faith and hope make a big difference as we face death, especially as we peer into the future. What would we do without them? We know the reality behind Paul's irony: "O death, where is thy victory? O death, where is thy sting?" At the time of our loved ones' deaths, though, we can pinpoint death's victory and sting precisely. All will be well. We believe that. But all is not well right away.

If deaths among other people cause us difficulties—and they do—even more problematic are thoughts about our own death. Thinking about dying scares most of us. As believers buoyed by the assurance conveyed in the death and resurrection of Jesus, we can say theoretically "to die is gain." But not practically.

Few, if any, of us are really ready to die. Life-breathing God, grant us comfort as we grieve the deaths of people whom we love.

And regarding ourselves, God, please don't let death scare the life out of us. If fears related to death persist, use them to scare the vibrancy of life into us.

We speak frankly to you and reach out for your help in the name of the Resurrection and the Life—not the events, but the person. Amen.

Depression

O Great Provider of peace and rest, Re-creator of our lives:

I am depressed. I am tired. I am tired of being depressed. When Jesus spoke compassionately of the weary and heavy-laden, he described me perfectly. My head is bent. My back aches. My chest is pushed down by invisible pressure and filled with indefinable anxiety. My eyes will close for sleep only stubbornly, but they readily fill with tears and weep. My feet feel like weights that make me shuffle rather than walk. My spirit sags. My heart is filled with melancholy at best, sadness at worst.

I don't like this, God. Who would? I cannot even remember happy days. I fail to rise to occasions of festivity with family and friends. I am self-conscious about my preoccupation with sorrow. I am unable to feel good about the future. I would like to just stay in bed a long time, sleep through difficult situations and eventually wake up refreshed with the realization that it was all a bad dream. But I know better. I must be honest even if I can't be happy. I want to feel better. I don't like this one bit, God.

What was it, God? What brought on this terrible depression? Grief? Was it the sudden loss of a relative? Was it the failure of a friendship? Despair? Was it a feeling of rejection? Was it betrayal by the one supposed to be my beloved? Was it watching the last child leave home? Fatigue? Or is this depression the predictable result of exhausting work done under tension and without relaxation? Is it the burnout condition caused by the pursuit of a relentless passion for success? Or anxiety? Is it the product of ceaseless worry? Is it the payoff of a radical insecurity? Maybe it is more physical than emotional or mental—a medically treatable, biochemical deficiency. Maybe, could it be?

Whatever its reasons for being, whatever the results of its manipulation of my feelings, my depression has not blunted my conviction about a need for divine help. I need you, God! Words cannot adequately convey my gratitude for your gracious acceptance of all people—including me—regardless of our situations. I find reassurance in the resurgence you accomplished in persons like Jonah and Jeremiah. Please do that to me.

How badly I long to look forward once again to the dawning of a new day, to be a part of an important relationship in which I have something to give, to sense meaning and fulfillment in my labor, to know a calm that is conducive to re-creation, and to smile—no, more than that, to laugh. Someday perhaps I can find all of that as a result of the gifts that come in good relationships with others. But for now, right now, I want to be sure that I find all that I need in all that is available from you. I know it will be enough. I am sure that you can help even the depressed. I am waiting, God, waiting for you, waiting and beginning to feel the first stirrings of—dare I believe it?—hope.

I beseech you in the name of the One who habitually gave hope to the hopeless, rest for the weary, and security for all eternity—and still does. Amen.

Dialogue

O God:
Your Holy Word brings forth our human words. You speak and
there is creation—warm sunshine, refreshing rain, a cooling breeze,
green grass, red roses, a world of wonder and enjoyment.

We speak and there is thanksgiving—praise to you for your
nature, gratitude for gifts to us, adoration to you for your accessible
holiness.

You speak and there is redemption—an invitation to confession,
an assurance of forgiveness, an offer of purpose, an incarnation of
love.

We speak and there is acceptance—we unload our guilt with a
sigh, grasp your forgiveness with delight, unite with the incarnate
Lord in commitment.

You speak and there is promise—words of comfort for grief, a
calming peace for anxiety, hope to overcome despair, your presence
for our loneliness.

We speak and there is faith—commitment to walk everywhere,
even through the dark shadows, in your name, trust to take up the
challenge of service, participation to strengthen the community of
faith called the church.

Your Holy Word brings forth our human words, O God.

> Yours is the kingdom—ours the service.
>
> Yours is the power—ours the trust.
>
> Yours is the glory forever—ours the joy of fellowship
>   with you.

We pray in the name of the Word who is both yours and ours—
Jesus the Christ. Amen.

9/29/96

Emotions

God of body, mind, and spirit:

As we begin to speak to you, we remember Isaiah, who went scurrying into your presence, dashing into the temple driven by a desire to speak to you. We remember because we know he found you. In that realization we take comfort. But God, we recall also that you found Isaiah—not only found him but looked with him at every part of his being.

Now we tremble in your presence. Surely you understand our uneasiness with the penetrating vision of your holy love. You know well that on the inside we are not just like we look on the outside. You are already aware that every time we worship you, we do so with mixed motives, multiple feelings, conflicting convictions, distracting emotions. In fact, we might just as well pray to you about all of this, since you see it so clearly anyway.

We are filled with many emotions, and attempts to worship you seem to intensify all of them—fear, anxiety, jealousy, pride, anger, love, happiness, sorrow. All of that is within us, God. When you see such a mix, you know why we have so much trouble listening to your word without distraction and offering ourselves singularly for your purposes. Address our emotions, O God.

Let us retain a healthy sense of fear that facilitates faith but be done with crippling fear as we hear your words "fear not."

You told us not to be anxious. Do you really understand— the business world, the competition? You do understand. Still our anxieties.

If we must be jealous, let us be jealous about big ideas and life-enriching patterns of behavior.

Is pride wrong, God? Enable us to be pleased with the personhood to which you have called us but dissatisfied with anything less.

You know our anger. We get mad. Enable us to channel the energy of our anger constructively.

Love is your gift. We know you affirm love within us. Enrich the love we have and increase our capacity for love so that we can love more.

Happiness and sorrow are all mixed up in us. We can almost laugh and cry in the same breath. Please join us in either and implant a hallelujah to yourself in both.

We do not pray to you as perfect persons. Rather we pray to you as people who want to be known and led by you. Enter our emotions that we may always worship and serve you with our emotions and our minds; in the name of the thinking and feeling Christ. Amen.

Enemies

Challenging, Reconciling God:

If we must have enemies, and they appear inevitable, let us have them for good reasons.

Individually, limit our enemies to those who
dislike our insistence upon integrity,
despise our persistence in service, and
reject our allegiance to the priority of grace.

As a church, may we have no enemies beyond those persons who
oppose the proclamation of the gospel,
resent compassionate outreach to all people,
reject any love, salvation, and assistance that is not
deserved,
condemn conscientious efforts to establish justice in
society and peace among the nations,
decry a ministry of reconciliation.

If we have enemies because of hypocrisy, cowardice, infidelity, abusiveness, insensitivity, bigotry, gracelessness, or dishonesty, forgive us, God.

If we must have enemies, let us have them for good reasons. Even then, though, enable us to relate to these people with efforts aimed at making them our friends.

We pray in the name of Jesus whose ministry consisted of making enemies friends—friends with each other, friends with you. Amen.

Enlightenment

Creator God, Source of all light:

Much as you declared, "Let there be light," and there was light, bring light into our darkened lives.

Our minds are dull.

Our consciences are weak.

Our wills are weary.

Even our hearing and seeing are no longer sharp.

It has not always been this way. Sometimes we have felt that all was well. We seemed to understand everything. Not now, though, God. At present, we don't understand anything.

Efforts aimed at good have been discouraged or defeated
    outright.

Doubts storm our faith and leave our convictions shaking.

Anger shows its power over reason.

Forgive us if we should not say it, but we even have cried
    out to you for help and heard nothing in response but
    the rattling of our voices.

Help us understand, O God. Help us understand
    when you seem to be distant,
    when you appear to be silent,
    when your way is so radically different from our way.

We need help, God. We need help from beyond ourselves—
    the enlightenment of your presence,
    the invigoration of your Spirit,
    the inspiration of your vision,
    the conviction of your Word.

O God, illumine our lives by the inviting, guiding, judging, redeeming light of your presence.

We pray for enlightenment through Jesus Christ our Lord who identified himself as the Light of the world. Amen.

Escape

O God:

I want to run. I don't know to where. I just want to run, to get away, to drop out, to be done with all of this heavy stuff that weighs me down.

If it can't be forever, then for a little while, I want to forget
worries prodded by economic problems,
pain caused by recent deaths,
conflict at every turn,
peer pressure that goes against my will,
insensitivity among people who know how to be sensitive,
appointments in the week ahead that cause anxieties right now,
thoughts that incite panic.

I know you understand. In the Bible, some of your best people sought escape from their plights. That's where I am. I want to hide, to allow my mind to slip into neutral, to free my spirit for unbounded soaring, to escape.

I must admit, though, that while the words of this prayer are forming, I have the strong feeling that it is not going to work. You know me better than I know myself. And I know you. Permanent retreat never qualifies as a divine provision.

If I ever do get up enough courage to try to run, please don't give up on me. In fact, even if I don't intend to, let me run into you.

Better still, bring to fulfillment within me the renewal that is always possible as a gift of your grace. Grant me satisfaction with the redemption and renewal that come from you, the redemption and renewal that I do not have to run anywhere to experience and that I can never totally run away from even if sometimes I am foolish enough to try.

These feelings I bring to you in the name of Jesus, the ultimate refuge. Amen.

Faith

O Faithful God:

Here we are praying for faith fully aware that it takes faith to pray. So what should we say? Must we ask for more faith? Can there be only a little faith? Or are not all attempts to quantify faith ridiculous? Isn't faith like life in the sense that either we have it or we don't?

Deliver us from confusion, God. Help us to know the difference between

faith and make-believe,
faith and imagination,
faith and optimism,
faith and magic.

Prevent us from turning faith into a means of escape from life, an excuse for ignorance, or a rationale for inactivity.

Right now, we want faith—mature faith.

Where faith is nonexistent, send your Spirit to move in the void, much like your Spirit moved over the face of the deep at the beginning of everything. Strike a spark of interest in faith within us. Compel a decision regarding faith from us. Nurture the exercise of faith by us.

Where faith already exists, deepen it. Nurture our faith, O God, by

enlightening our minds,
sensitizing our emotions,
increasing our actions,
strengthening our wills, and
making complete our obedience.

We long for faith with a passion akin to that of a loving mother searching for a lost child. We hunger and thirst for faith the way people deprived of food and drink seek sustenance.

Give us faith, faithful God. Allow faith to be born in us, to grow in us, and to find expression through us. Fill our faith with joy and certainty—excitement as if this were the first day of our Christian pilgrimage and conviction as if it were the last.

We pray in the name of the pioneer of our faith as well as its author and finisher. Amen.

Familiarity

God of tradition and innovation, the new and the old:

Our spirits are jaded by familiarity. In relation to Christianity, we sense that we have heard it all, seen it all, and done it all before. So now we operate more on our assumptions than your revelation.

We open the Bible with presuppositions. We limit your leadership by certain conditions.

Visit us with freshness, God.

Enable us to hear your Word as if for the first time.

Encourage us to follow your leadership as if on the front edge of a new adventure.

Open our minds as well as our ears. Grant us powers of perception in our spirits as well as in our eyes.

Speak to us.

Enlighten us.

Lead us.

Make all things new.

Both our confessions and our requests are made through the One whom to know in faith is to follow as a new creation. Amen.

Family

O God, whom to be with is to be at home:

The very idea of family was born out of the fellowship of the Holy Trinity. We thank you for the general idea and its embodiment in specific persons.

Whether through natural birth or by means of adoption, you have brought persons together to love and care for one another. We express gratitude for such nurture.

Understanding God, please do not hear us as unappreciative if we confess that families have problems. Certainly that is not your fault. You have given us good models. You have guided our steps. But there are problems even among families who worship you regularly.

We have the capacity (sometimes a strong tendency) to mess up that which you have intended as good. Brothers and sisters quarrel with each other. Husbands and wives fail to get along. Grandparents are forgotten. Cousins become vicious competitors. Family members even abuse one another—mostly by manipulation and language, but sometimes by physical and psychological violence.

O God, help us—

Enable us to recognize and deal with the fatigue that
    allows us to destroy our loved ones.
Spare us that torrid, selfish drive to success that causes
    us to ignore and hurt those with whom we live.
Still the surges of jealousy and competitiveness that fill
    our lives but empty meaning from our relationships.
Teach us understanding, patience, forgiveness, and
    reconciliation.
Help us love again.

We desire for ourselves and request from you families that emulate, at least in part, your family, O God. Amen.

Fatigue

Do you not ever get tired, God? I am amazed at the constancy of your grace and the fidelity of your love. I don't see how you do it.

I get real tired. Sometimes my fatigue is related to study and work, to a loss of sleep and a lack of rest. But sometimes the fatigue is in my soul.

I grow weary of knocking myself out to do something good
    and seeing the unstinting success of evil.

I feel like I have been carrying a five-hundred-pound load
    on my back for days when my prayers seem to do no more
    than fall to the floor.

I get tired of exercising faith and seeking more and more
    assurance that it makes a difference.

Soul fatigue is terrible. Pain pervades the body as anxiety dominates the spirit. Rest does not come, cannot come, even when activities cease, silence prevails, and I can lie down on a bed.

I plead for a realization of the rest that can come only from you.

Enable me to know emotional rest as well as physical
    relaxation.

Give me peace in my mind and soul.

Fill my heart with new life as you forgive the sins that have
    marred the days of the past.

O God, I am in awe of your eternal energy. I praise your enduring care. I give thanks for your tireless grace.

Minister to me out of your divine nature.

In moments of unusual gladness, spur my spirit to soar as
    if upon the wings of eagles.

In hours of constant but fulfilling labor, strengthen me to
    run and not be weary.

At other times, more difficult and draining, filled with
    relentless fatigue, assist me so I can walk and not faint.

I pray to you in the name of Jesus who offers to all a sabbath rest. Amen.

Focus

Loving God:

Why is it so difficult for us to keep our attention focused on you?
Even in worship our minds wander. Our thoughts stray.

We talk about blessings and think of our achievements.

We speak of praise to you and ponder our self-worth.

We start to pray for others and suddenly all we can see are
our own needs, fears, and difficulties.

At any one moment, multiple interests crowd our minds and vie for
attention.

We care about poverty and think about play.

We acknowledge a concern about world hunger and quickly
drop it to concentrate on a new book we want to read.

We begin to worship privately, and immediately distractions
divert us from meditating on your holy presence.

A part of the difficulty resides in our intolerance of mystery.
Mastery over life seems within our grasp. We feel that every problem
can be traced to an explainable cause and treated with efforts that
guarantee a successful resolution. Thus, we have trouble thinking for
long about you.

For an education we go to the academy.

For food we shop at supermarkets.

For suffering we visit a physician.

For success we think positively.

For fellowship we buy entertainment tickets.

For forgiveness we say to a colleague, "I beg your pardon."

For faith and hope we suck in air, stiffen our backs, and
forge ahead as courageous captains of our souls.

Thinking of you and you alone is not easy for us. Good God, make
our vision single, our focus solitary. As we look at creation, give us a
vision of the Creator. As we request redemption, let us see the
Redeemer.

Then save us from allowing that vision to slip away. If our minds
must wander, help them to wander in your works. If our eyes must
stray, help them to stray within your glory. Enable us to set our sights
on you and to sustain that concentration until we are moved to
worship and service through a life of love.

We seek to be done with fragmentation and to know wholeness, to
avoid confusion and to experience enduring concern.

O God, establish within us
> the joy of an uncluttered vision of your holiness,
> the happiness of a single-minded devotion to your presence,
> the fulfillment of complete obedience to your will.

We pray in the name of Jesus who helps us see you, understand you, love you, and serve you. Amen.

Food

God of the great banquet:

We give you thanks for food not because we have plenty to eat while others are empty, but because with nourishment come strength and energy for service—for sharing skills, information, and resources that all may have food.

With every bite of food we take, we are conscious of being bountifully blessed. With every mouthful of food we chew, make us aware of our food-related responsibility in the world community: We are blessed in order to be a blessing.

We pray in the name of the Bread of Life. Amen.

Forgiveness

O Great, Forgiving God:

Our identity as sinners and our need for forgiveness are more than matters of doctrine. They are facts of personal experience. We are sinners who need forgiveness. The depth of that realization inspires the heights of our thanksgiving.

Thanks be to you, O God, for the grace gift of forgiveness.
> You love us when we are not lovable.
> You do not give up on us when we give up on ourselves.
> You provide us strength when our energy is gone.
> You offer us direction when we wander about in confusion.
> You affirm our worth when we feel worthless.
> You assure us of forgiveness when it is certain that we
>   will sin again.
> You respond with life when our words and actions invite
>   death.

Thanks be to you, O God, for the grace gift of forgiveness.

A longing complements our thanksgiving—a desire to be able to extend to others the kind of forgiveness we have received from you. Please help us with our forgiveness as you receive our words of gratitude for your forgiveness.

We speak to you in the name of your Son who, as a perfectly innocent person, became sin in order that we, the true sinners, might know forgiveness and have the opportunity to live as new creations. Amen.

Gifts

O God, Giver of all that is good:

We know what to give a newborn baby, but what are we to do with a king? And what if the king is a baby? Diapers, powder, and rattles seem as inappropriate for a king as do gold, silver, and perfume for a baby.

We know what to give to a dying man, but what are we to do with a king? And what if the king is a dying man? A shroud to wear, a spot for entombment, and a mixture of oil and spices with which to anoint the body seem as inappropriate for a king about to rise from the dead as do jewelry, timepieces, and cologne for a man who will never breathe again.

O God, if you find as acceptable the gift of our lives to your Son, we offer now our lives. We desire

> to love him,
> to grow with him,
> to serve him,
> to honor him.

Here are our lives, O God. We pray that they will be acceptable offerings in your sight and valid gifts to your Son the king; in his name. Amen.

God

Sovereign, Compassionate God:

When we attempt to speak of your nature in prayer, we end up stammering for words and scratching our heads while searching for appropriate phrases. We are without precedent, analogies, or metaphors to aid us. You are as much unlike us as we are unable to bring in your kingdom by ourselves. With amazement, we recognize in you

power made perfect in weakness,
love more devoted to giving than to receiving,
holiness that embraces the world,
justice that is a servant to grace,
death that leads to life.

Save us from all speculations that attempt to confine you to the categories of finite existence. Remind us that we are created in your image, not you in our image.

Lead us into ever greater insights into your nature by increasing our understanding and devotion to the supreme revelation of yourself in Jesus Christ. As subjects of his lordship and citizens of your kingdom, we pledge ourselves to the pursuit of new truths about your nature through our worship and service.

We pray in the name of the One who bore the stamp of your likeness. Amen.

Good Friday

O God:

How could, how dare, anyone call this day "good"?

The earth shakes with injustice. Darkened skies form a backdrop for despicable evil. Your Son screams of abandonment.

What good is here?

We crucified perfect love.
We killed One who came to give life.
We nailed to a tree the ultimate liberator who desired
to set us free.

Pardon my obstinacy, God, but I fail to see any good anywhere on this Friday.

Still the rage within our world and the panic within our hearts that we may hear your voice and learn the good that underlies what looks to us like a terrible orgy of evil.

Good *is* here. Once we are in touch with you, we see it. Sear the good into our souls. Establish it in our hearts so that we will never forget it.

>The fact that you still speak to us indicates you have not
>given up on us. That is good.

>You took the worst action possible and brought redemption
>out of it. That is good. It was not a one-time
>occurrence. Even now you take tragic situations and wring
>some admirable good out of them.

>At Golgotha you demonstrated that you will love us even
>while we try to shove you out of our lives. That is good.

>You did for us that which we could never do for ourselves,
>that which we need most if we are ever to really be the
>persons you created us to be. That is good.

>You revealed that sometimes you offer forgiveness to us
>though we don't request it. That is real good.

O God, the good is there. The name of the day fits—Good Friday. The good just seems so distant. And so difficult. So shrouded by the blackness of grief caused by Jesus' death. So encrusted with layer after layer of hardened guilt.

But it is there. God, you have helped us to see good where good did not seem possible. And you do it time and time again.

We praise you, O God, as we thank you for this day and for the events that made (that make) it good. We offer profound gratitude for the hope that is born in the recognition that you can take a bad Friday—a really, unbelievably bad Friday—and fill it with so much grace that history enshrines it as Good Friday.

Our prayer is made through the One who on that day declared, "It is finished," as he commended himself to you. Amen.

Gospel

O God, I am full up with bad news. It seems like that is the only kind of news making the rounds recently.

My craving for good news is so ravenous that I am scared by it. I fear that, if they sound good enough, I might accept promises that I know can't be kept, that I could listen to someone make up news if that brought me pleasure, that I could cast my lot with the dispensers of superficial joy. Please save me from such folly. I long for good news.

I am well past ready to hear again the assurances that grow out of your love—not made-up words captured in ragged clichés, not shallow generalities, but real truths bearing substance and power. I am listening, God.

I need faith. You have made faith possible, providing a
redemptive pioneer in faith and excellent models of faith.

I need love. You have promised love, an everlasting love
evident in deeds as well as in words.

I need hope. You can lift our heads as well as our hearts, offering the
assurance that nothing around people can defeat the hope that you
plant within people.

I know that I am not alone in my pursuit of the Good News. Countless others can be blessed by the gospel as well. So I want to pray for the spread of the gospel. Is that audacious, God? I hope not. My prayer springs not from any lack of confidence in your power but from a concern for an effective ministry of the gospel among your people.

Send the gospel to every person on earth, O God. Let the Good News spread with enthusiasm and joy. I want to be a part of that movement, God. I want to serve as a messenger of the gospel.

I pray for wisdom beyond my own wisdom as I seek to commend
Christ to others.

I pray for strength beyond my own strength as I strive to be
faithful to the task of telling the truth in love.

I pray for vision beyond my own vision as I try to discover
new ways to embrace a world and to pervade its
communities with Christian proclamation.

I pray for courage beyond my own courage so that I can speak the
Good News with conviction even in the face of threats of
retribution.

O God, fill me with the Good News of the gospel and use me in the sharing of this Good News with others.

I pray in the name of Jesus, who is the gospel. Amen.

Grace

God of grace:

Your grace-filled goodness staggers us. We are accustomed to judgment, denunciation, retaliation, and retribution. We react to evil with harsh actions aimed at a defense of good. After all, someone must protect righteousness. Your grace-full response to sinful persons is incongruent. A total surprise.

We offer thanks for your grace. As we do, however, we have to admit that we don't deserve it. Judgment is good enough for us. Even punishment. We do continue to praise you for your grace, though, realizing that if it were deserved, it would not be grace.

Somehow, God, take the unguarded enthusiasm with which we receive grace and use it to sustain our efforts to serve as instruments of grace. Toward that end, clear our minds of all thoughts about merit and rid our attitudes of every intention to inflict judgment.

Keep before us the truth that the grace we administer to others will always be like the grace you offer to us—

never deserved,

always costly,

never easy,

always risky,

never understandable,

always controversial.

Neither time nor circumstances will ever be right for grace. Remind us that if they were, something other than grace would suffice.

Close our ears to comments from others as you reassure us that grace will always look

ill-advised,

foolish,

soft on sin,

ridiculous,

hilarious.

Accept our thanks as beneficiaries of grace, O God. Create within us a commitment to live as servants of grace.

We pray as we seek to behave in the name of the One who embodied "grace upon grace." Amen.

Hallelujah

Great God Almighty:

Did you hear that? The hallelujah? It was for you. A choir was singing the biblical words that George Frederick Handel so magnificently set to music. Hallelujahs explode joyfully. Some of us were repressing the urge to shout hallelujah, though we were whispering the word under our breath.

What we have learned to sing in hymns and oratorios, what we have decided to say in litanies and prayers, we now seek to live in all situations—in *all* situations.

"Comfort ye my people"—hallelujah!

"The glory of the Lord shall be revealed"—hallelujah!

"He is like a refiner's fire"—hallelujah!

"Unto us a child is born"—hallelujah!

"Fear not"—hallelujah!

"He shall speak peace"—hallelujah!

"He shall give you rest"—hallelujah!

"He hath borne our griefs and carried our sorrows"—hallelujah!

"Blessing and honor, glory and power be unto him"—hallelujah!

"He shall reign forever and ever"—hallelujah!

O Mighty God:

What we request in invocation, we discover as your benediction—a hallelujah—a hallelujah that can be

shouted beside a manger,

muttered through tears under a cross,

exclaimed breathlessly in the open passageway of an
empty tomb,

heralded vigorously in our hometowns,

embraced thoroughly in our lives,

shared compassionately throughout the world.

We accept your gift of a hallelujah. We take it up. Indeed, we commit our lives to live according to its spirit until your kingdom comes and your will is done on earth as in heaven so that we then can join with all creation in declaring the Christ as King of kings and Lord of lords. Forever. And ever. Hallelujah. Hallelujah! Amen.

Help

God of the mountains and valleys:

Trusting the inspired word of the psalmist, who asserts that our help comes from the Lord, we turn to you with a plea for help. Help, please

that student so burdened down with work and plagued by a sense of loneliness that she is about to quit school and give up on herself;

that young man who is struggling for identity and worrying that he is neither worthy nor capable of relationships;

that chairperson of the board for whom work has become a nearly intolerable chore because of the need to give attention to personal problems;

that office worker who cannot concentrate on clerical skills because of the threat imposed by medical problems;

that friend who is fighting with doubts and seeking a stronger faith;

that family member who feels no love, sees no purpose, and experiences no fulfillment in daily life.

As we pray for help for others, we also seek your help for ourselves. It is all we can do to keep from screaming, "Help!" We need your help so badly. None of us has life completely all together. We need you—your love, your guidance, your forgiveness, your grace. O God, yes, most of all we need your grace.

At times we have experienced what the psalmist declared. Our help does come from you. We long to experience that help again. Please, God, help us now.

We ask for help in the name of the perfect helper. Amen.

Who is the author and Giver of Hope ....

Amen

47

Holy Spirit

O Triune God:
>For the gift of your Holy Spirit, we offer praise and thanks.
>Send your Spirit to guide us—
>>teaching us how to live as well as what to believe,
>>leading us through dark valleys as well as along sunny slopes,
>>directing us toward persons in need and places of mission,
>>enabling us to dream, to venture, and to risk in your name.
>Send your Spirit to strengthen us—
>>enriching our joy in discipleship,
>>giving us courage to remain faithful to our convictions and loyal in our moral commitments,
>>binding our covenants with one another and with you.
>Send your Spirit to comfort us—
>>calming our anxieties,
>>stilling our worries,
>>granting us your loving presence when we feel alone,
>>drying our tears,
>>preventing prolonged grief,
>>assuring us of the resources of faith.

O God of Pentecost, let us live forever in your Spirit—guided, strengthened, and comforted. And may the Christ who taught us of the Spirit be our Lord forever. Amen.

Holy Week

O God of revelation and redemption, honor and humility:
We speak reluctantly. We step lightly. Our souls rise up on tiptoes.
We sense that we stand on holy ground. Our hearts pound against our
chests. Nervously we shuffle our feet. We are not accustomed to such
a scene. Seldom, if ever, do we see so clearly the rape of goodness
and the brutality of disobedience set against the disarming depth and
well-nigh incredible breadth of true love.

As we reflect again on Jesus' last week in Jerusalem, past and
present merge. We keep seeing our faces in the crowd. Occasionally,
we think we hear our voices amid the shouts of those people clus-
tered around Jesus. We grow very uncomfortable sensing that the
major issues of Holy Week are as much a part of our world today as
they were over two thousand years ago in the dusty streets of Jerusalem. The way those folks treated Jesus is not nearly so significant as
the way we treat Jesus now.

We don't see anything in Jesus' passion that is totally unfamiliar
to us. Most of what happened in Jerusalem we know experientially.

At times our emotions have fluctuated so wildly that words
of betrayal were voiced in almost the same breath as
words of acceptance.
We have questioned authority.
We have grown very uncomfortable with the conflict between
our avowed allegiance to Jesus and our necessary loyalty
to political institutions.
We are sure that we have brought clutter to the house of
God, sometimes reducing matters of faith to commodities
of commerce.

None of the crucial players in that drama of redemption are all that
different from us. Except Jesus.

Like Peter, we have wanted redemption without sacrifice,
greatness without servanthood, and fellowship without the
washing of feet.
Like Judas, we have tried to force your hand, to reshape
the ministry of your Son to accommodate our desires.
Like Pilate, we have wavered in decision making and failed
to do the good we knew to do.

That is why, as much as we desire the spiritual benefits of this
week, we dread making the personal pilgrimage through it once

more. Invariably, we find out much about ourselves that we would just as soon not know. It happens every year.

Ready or not, though, we are committed to making the journey to the cross again this year. This time through it we want badly to be able to stay with Jesus until the end—identifying with him as intimately and as publicly on Good Friday as we do on Palm Sunday. Perhaps with the genuine repentance and overwhelming forgiveness that are so much a part of the week, we can do it.

O God, help us to welcome into our lives the One who entered Jerusalem riding on a donkey. As time wears on and fidelity to him becomes tough, enable us to reject the strong temptation to push him away and to pin him down somewhere beyond the entrance to our lives. God, strengthen us that we may celebrate your salvation appropriately. We want to shout to Jesus, "Hosanna. Blessed is he who comes in the name of the Lord," and make it stick.

We shout hosanna and pray in his name. Amen.

Honesty

O God, Good God:

Finally! At long last we are engaged in a conversation in which we can be honest. Totally honest.

We are so very weary of surface emotions, meaningless gibberish, and superficial relationships. You know our situations, even our spoken lines.

Worried to death about balancing this month's budget, we
paste on a smile with a hope of making another sale.
Feeling absolutely frantic over decisions to be made, we
repress the chaos and present an image of calmness.
A friend hurts us. We don't understand. We want to retreat into
solitude and protect ourselves from more pain, but when the
friend asks how we are, we muster the effort to say, "Just fine."
We are tired of faking enthusiasm, saying what we do not mean, selling out our integrity for acceptability. We will be honest before you, O God.

Some of us are mad at you—we do not know why you do not
demonstrate your sovereignty more. Recent deaths, present
illnesses, awkward situations could have been avoided.
Some of us are disappointed with you—we thought you would

make it possible for pain not to hurt, criticisms not to sting,
love not to be so vulnerable.

Some of us just need to hear a word from you. Let us know
you are near or here, that you still honor commitment, that
you continue to comfort grief.

Great God, this feels so good—to be honest, to hold nothing back,
to open our hearts and minds to you, not to measure every word or
guard every emotion. In Scripture you promise us that truth is a part of
your very nature. Thus, please hear us and respond to us. Speak to us,
show us, lead us into truth. Reduce our concern for what others think.
Somehow we want to be more authentic. Mold us in that manner. We
want to be the persons you created us to be.

We pray in the name of the One known as the Truth. Amen.

Hospital

O God:

"You will only have to stay in the hospital two days, three at the
most," the doctor told me. First, I froze. Now I have panicked. The
hospital epitomizes so much of what I dislike: illness, weakness,
dependency, vulnerability. Those are the feelings.

But I also hate the tangibles associated with hospitals: ugly gowns,
needles, a bed pan, and endless tests.

Then, too, I shudder as I anticipate a biopsy. Worse still, though,
are gnawing anxieties about a discovery that would give rise to the
possibility of life-disrupting surgery.

My feelings have nothing to do with a lack of faith or an absence of
hope. My faith is intact. Hope is secure. I just don't like hospitals with
their difficult diagnoses, surgical procedures, physical therapy, and
orders for recuperation.

Surely you understand, God.

I am confident that your divine will is for human health. If, *if* a
hospital can be one of your instruments for dealing with disease and
bringing health, as I suspect, I know, it can, I still will not like it, but I
will, as best I can, give thanks for it. And I will go to the hospital and
become a patient.

Thanks for promising to be there with me. I love you, God. I just
don't like the hospital as a meeting place.

I pray in the name of Jesus who received care as well as gave it.
Amen.

House Blessing

Loving God, who created us for relationships and set us among families:

Thank you for the lives and love that fill this house. Well aware that we can dedicate minds, wills, and hearts better than bricks, mortar, and lumber, we speak to you now not only about this house but also about its residents who desire that this place become a home. Through their compassion and hospitality, make this house a refuge in which friends can gather for fellowship and believers can assemble for encouragement in their faith.

Give all who pass through these doors a sense of welcome and an invitation to draw strength from the devotion and commitment that fill the lives of the family members who fill this house.

We pray for times of boundless happiness, joyful laughter, and mutual fulfillment. We pray as well for moments of stress, conditions of sadness, and even for occasions of tears. In both times—exultation and sadness—may faith and its resourcefulness for hope be obvious to all who come here.

As a site of important decision-making, transform this house into an altar that your divine wisdom may prevail and your divine will may direct.

God, bless this house and those who live within its walls. May this prayer of dedication be complemented in the days ahead by prayers of confession, intercession, praise, thanksgiving, and commitment.

You have taught us that the family can be a crucible of the kingdom and the home a symbol of our union with you. Allow this house and this family to be faithful to such images.

O God, bless this house and this family even as we dedicate both to your glory; through Jesus Christ who made us realize that to be in your presence is to be at home. Amen.

Hunger

God of manna in the wilderness and fish and bread on the mountainside:

We pray for people who are hungry. As we do so, we praise you for the richness of your love, and we confess to you the inadequacy of our understanding.

We have trouble knowing what it is like to be hungry—really hungry. Most of us have known hunger pains only temporarily. We have not been sickened and crippled by a lack of calories.

We also have difficulty understanding the whole matter of destiny—why we were born among bounty while others came into existence amid the pathos of starvation. We do realize that our fortunate status has nothing to do with our goodness or their evil or with some preferential treatment in your love.

Confessing our lack of understanding, we pray for hungry people.
Fan whatever spark of hope may still be alive within them.
Touch their numbness with your love that they may know they matter.
Send the sunshine and the rains so that seeds can burst open and life-giving fruits and vegetables can come from the soil, that more people may eat.
Strengthen and guide those organizations at work to feed hungry people, to alter agricultural policies, to produce more food in sites of traditional scarcity.
Blunt the attempts of those who would jeopardize hungry people's lives by using food for political and economic advantages.
Encourage those people who are trying to live on a little food and work toward the production of more. Help them learn how to plant and to reap and to preserve.
Prevent any hungry person from confusing economic conditions with your divine will. Don't let any child living with hunger feel unloved or unwanted by people who follow Christ.

O God, the more we pray for hungry people, the more we realize the need to pray for ourselves. Create a hunger in our souls! Make us ravenous for social justice and international peace. Give us an insatiable desire for righteousness and responsibility. Cause us to long for experiences of sharing your resources and ourselves for the betterment of others. Give us courage to examine our lifestyles. If we take from others by claiming too much for ourselves, forgive us and change us. Nurture compassion and generosity among us that we may share thoughtfully and give sacrificially. Prevent us from being content with the offering of a word about love when someone needs a piece of bread, but keep us also from trying to substitute the gift of a piece of bread when someone needs the gift of love.

Resourceful God, we pray for all who hunger—
> those who hunger and thirst after righteousness,
> those who hunger for fellowship,
> those who hunger for salvation, and
> those who hunger for meaning as well as those who hunger
> for food.

Feed them, God. Feed them through us.

As we give thanks for daily bread for ourselves, we pray for the grace to share that there may be bread for all the world; in the name of the Bread of Life. Amen.

Hurt

O God, whose Son is known as "Man of Sorrows":

Today I am hurting bad! (Oh, I know that's only a slang expression, but it conveys the life-smothering, soul-bending weight of my hurt.) I am hurting bad.

No sooner have I made that confession than comes the realization that I am not alone. Maybe personal feelings blur my perspective. Yet when I look around sensitively, everyone appears to be hurting to one degree or another.

I pray for all who hurt, God. I pray that they will know an easing of their hurts.

> The mother and father whose son has turned on them in
> inexplicable anger and stormed away from home.
> The young woman who this week received notice that she
> would not be accepted for graduate studies.
> The rag-garbed man (who could guess his age?) covered
> with newspapers, sound asleep on a park bench.
> The middle-aged mother whose doctor gave her a bad report on
> a recent biopsy.
> The budding athlete who has been told he cannot

participate again in competitive sports.

The hungry children who do not understand the pain in
their stomachs or, worse still, why no one seems to care
that it's there.

The man who saw the love of his life turn her back on
his love and walk away from him, scattering behind her
the debris of his broken dreams.

Hurt takes so many forms and finds expression in such diverse
symptoms that we sometimes try to catalog it by degrees. Save us
from such irrelevant speculation, O God, and deliver us from the
well-meaning but counterproductive suggestions on how loud to
scream or how low to bend. No one can tell anyone else about that.

I am well aware of how your children in the past handled their
hurts—

David weeping over the actions of Absalom and then even
more over his own actions;

Job struggling to continue blessing your name while
wanting to cry "foul" as he reeled from one tragedy
after another despite his righteousness;

Jonah fretting over the repentance of a city that cast a
shadow of doubt on his prophetic competence;

Peter scurrying into the shadows, devastated by his
failure of nerve and faith;

Judas swinging limply from a tree—having given in to the
darkness that flooded his heart despite the light of a
Passover moon.

Like us, some brought hurt upon themselves while others became
victims of a hurt that seemed unjustifiable and inexplicable.

But what are they to do now? What am I to do?

O God, make me and all who hurt recipients of the ministry of
your Son. Though unable to explain how, I do believe that by his
hurts our hurts can be healed. Help me so to trust in Christ and to
experience his healing that I can one day look back and give you
thanks even for this day. But you know I cannot do that yet.

My prayer is to scream for help or to plead, "Come, Lord Jesus,"
and it is offered in his name. Amen.

Intimidation

God of faith and hope:

We seek to be your people today. Keep us from being intimidated by either the past or the future.

When in retrospect we review the pilgrimages of our predecessors in the faith, we are tempted toward unreality. Recognizing their accomplishments and faithfulness, we forget or overlook their pains, failures, and setbacks. Seeing them as more than human, we decide we can never be like them or never labor as they labored. Keep us in touch with truth, God. You enable your work to be done by people just like us.

We can be faithful even though we have known fear.

We can achieve goals even though we have desired to give up.

We can do good even though we have done evil.

We can be instruments of your grace even if we see ourselves as unworthy.

Keep us from being intimidated by either our past or our future.

When we assess all that needs to be done and the gifts required to do it, we are tempted to shrink back. We see all that is wrong in our lives as individuals and the weaknesses in our institutions. We feel more prone to despair than to hope. Redeem us by your truth.

Intentionally you have called us. We are your divine choices for carrying out the church's mission in the present. Those whom you call, you strengthen. Those whom you send out, you accompany. We are not exceptions. Thus, allow our commitment to you to be encouraged by your confidence in us. Informed—not intimidated—by our past, challenged—not intimidated—by our future, in this present moment we offer ourselves to you in faith and in hope in the name of the One who unites the past and the future, Jesus Christ our Lord. Amen.

Invocation

Omniscient, Omnipotent, Omnipresent God:

Dare we invoke your name and invite your presence on any
occasion? Is that our prerogative? We're not sure. Should we seek
special attention from you right now?

> Certainly not if we are unaware of your constant gifts to us
> and if we are devoid of gratitude.

> Certainly not if we fail to take seriously our sins before
> you and fail to request forgiveness from you.

> Certainly not unless we have come with openness, ready to
> risk being molded by your Spirit, instructed by your Word,
> and led by your Son.

> Certainly not if being here is a way of shutting out others
> and escaping ministry rather than seeking to be more
> sensitive to others and more effective in ministry.

But God, we seek your attention. We request your presence. We
desire an encounter with you. So we invoke your name.

> We have come aware of your blessings and eager to give
> thanks.

> We have come aware of our sins and humble in our requests
> for forgiveness.

> We have come completely open to your re-creative presence.

> We have come aware of others' needs to which we must minister
> but aware also of our own needs for ministry—ministry that
> only you can provide.

We are eager to meet you, O God. Or to be met by you. Hear,
then, our invocation. Out of your grace, come to us

> to comfort and disturb,
> to bless and demand,
> to heal and challenge,
> to minister and make us minister.

Please come now, God. We are ready. We wait and pray in the
Christ's name. Amen.

Jesus

O God from whom came our elder brother Jesus:

We hear the name of Jesus, ponder the ministry of Jesus, and discover multiple reactions, some of which please us and some that disturb us.

Obviously, we sense profound gratitude. How often our hearts go racing to Bethlehem so we can elbow our way in among the straggling wanderers gathered there to see the face of perfect love. A laughter of happiness rings out as we experience forgiveness and realize redemption. Looking back, we are thankful for Jesus.

But now, God, now comes frightening honesty. We do not feel comfortable injecting the name of Jesus into all our conversations. Just to speak the name outside the fellowship of the church causes a dis-ease within us. Maybe we have seen too many media proclamations that we question: a Jesus T-shirt, a bumper sticker telling us to honk if we love Jesus, some clownish-looking character who sits in the end zone of a football stadium and holds up a sign that declares "Jesus saves." We do not want to be seen as fanatics—Jesus freaks or religious weirdos.

However, God, we need wisdom from you to know where and how Jesus fits into life today. We do not want abuses of his name to prevent the right uses of his name. We sense that his ministry belongs as much among us as it did among our forbears in Galilee.

Open our lives to Jesus that he may come to us—by the seashore, in the marketplace, around the dinner table.

Strengthen our attentiveness to Jesus that we may incorporate into our lives his teachings about love, grace, and service.

Set before our consciences Jesus' convictions about personal worth, human equality, and the necessity of integrity, forgiveness, and compassion in all interpersonal relationships.

Create within us a boldness and loyalty that keep us from trying to push Jesus out of our world by crucifying him afresh.

Grant to us the abandonment that comes from true trust in Jesus that we may race to the risen Lord, dance in his presence, and then embrace his love and power forever.

O God, we pledge allegiance to Jesus the pioneer in faith, the pathfinder whose way we follow and in whose name we pray. Amen.

Joke

Happiness-giving God, inspiration for Sarah's laughter, creator of the playful sea monster, and celebrant of the joy that fills heaven when one sinner repents:

We are prone to play pranks on others, to find pleasure in jokes at someone else's expense. Give us discernment to know what is appropriate, so that any laughter we cause can be enjoyed by everyone without violating the dignity and personhood of anyone.

Preserve the seriousness with which we view the responsibilities of our lives, but stop us short of taking ourselves so seriously that we cannot laugh at ourselves whether alone or with others. Thank you for creating within us a sense of humor.

We realize that when we try to play a fast one on you—acting as if you do not exist, ignoring or disobeying your word—the joke will always be on us. And *that* one will be no laughing matter. Grant us the good sense to avoid such nonsense.

Instill within us such faith, mark our character with such morality, and so establish our actions of fidelity that the ultimate joke of the ages is on Satan as sinners continue to repent and laughter resounds through heaven to the absolute delight of all your people.

We pray in the name of the One who gives us the last laugh, even over death. O death where is your sting? Amen.

Joy

Eternal Author of joy:

We cling to every promise of joy like a nonswimmer clutching a life raft in deep, turbulent waters. We want joy—God, you know how we want joy. So desperate is our quest for it that we have looked in many wrong places and even attempted to purchase it much as we would buy toothpaste. You know all this about us. You know us.

We are strugglers. Some of us are attempting to resolve major questions, to make decisions with long-term implications. We long for joy.

We are bargainers. Some of us are seeking to close deals, to sign contracts, to finalize agreements in which the stakes are high, the financial consequences awesome. We want joy.

We are lovers. Some of us are starving for long-term relationships. So great are our needs that we are easily deceived. Help us distinguish between subtle manipulation and legitimate motivation. Do not let us confuse sexual gratification with personal communication. Prevent us from holding back anything in the name of love and from giving too much under the guise of love. We seek joy.

We are workers. Some of us are mistaking busyness for meaningfulness. You know that some of us hate what we are doing, but cannot stand the thought of making a change. Others of us try to substitute what we are doing for quality of being. Please give us joy.

We are sinners. Some of us are sensing an almost unbearable defeat because we cannot get on top of our wrongdoings. We intend good but do evil. Whatever thoughts we have had about sinning bravely have vanished in futility. We desire forgiveness—forgiveness with joy.

Strugglers, bargainers, lovers, workers, sinners—we are all seekers of joy. We open ourselves to your good gift and promise to be good stewards of what we receive; in the name of the One whom to know is to find joy. Amen.

Kiss

Compassionate God who kisses all creation with the tender care needed for life:

From your Holy Word we have learned that a kiss can be a joyful expression of love or a despicable act of disobedience. Preserve for us the former and save us from the latter.

Encourage us never to think ourselves too old to kiss the persons we love and never to behave so immaturely as to make a kiss an act of irresponsibility. Save us from ever being shamed by the separation of a kiss from devotion and make us forever unashamed of demonstrations of this sign of love.

We pray in the name of the One who died as a result of a kiss of betrayal and who, as the resurrected Lord, inspired the practice of a holy kiss within the family of faith. Amen.

Laughter

How we want to laugh again, O God. Really laugh.

We are weary of politely smiling at people when everything within us frowns.

For far too long we have faked joy, forced laughs to be socially acceptable, chuckled so as not to appear odd when someone tells a supposedly funny story. Most of the time, feigning laughter seems easier than explaining somberness.

We are fed up with all that. We want to laugh. We long to feel a laugh welling up within us—

> a laugh that we could not repress if we tried,
> a laugh that covers our faces,
> a laugh that convulses our bodies,
> a laugh that clears our minds,
> a laugh that relaxes tense nerves,
> a laugh that nurtures the freedom of our spirits,
> a laugh that sends tears streaming down our cheeks and
>   welcome pains stabbing at our sides,
> a laugh so important to express that what others think
>   about it does not matter.

God, we want to experience a laughter that seems like it will never stop, a laughter of complete hilarity, a laughter that leaves us physically weak and breathing heavily, but happy—very, very happy.

Thankfully, you know well what we mean, O laughing God. With divine delight, you shaped the playful sea monster, saw to it that old Sarah became pregnant, filled the apostle Paul with such confident joy that he could jest even with death itself, and, in your image, created people who possess not only the capacity for sobriety but a funny bone.

Please, God of joy, enable us to laugh again.

We make our request through the festive Jesus. Amen.

Law (Civil)

Divine Author of law and Redeemer by grace:
As we ponder the primacy of law in our society, give us wisdom—
wisdom to see law as servant not master,
wisdom to accept law as guide not god,
wisdom to recognize law as the will of a civil majority
and not necessarily the embodiment of biblical morality,
wisdom to understand law as worthy of study but unworthy
of worship.
As we celebrate the role of law in our community, local and
national, give us vision—
vision to reevaluate historic positions and to write new
legislation when needed,
vision to assure that legal precepts honor equality, to
settle for no less than justice, and to facilitate peace,
vision to labor at laws that balance blessings and
responsibilities and that enact restrictions only to enhance
liberties,
vision to persist in efforts to enforce laws that insist
on the kind of good actions for which we would lack
courage or will if left alone.
As we consider our own relation to the law personally, fill us with
sensitivity—
sensitivity to the importance of pardon as well as
punishment,
sensitivity to the difference between the civil and the
spiritual—the necessity of law and the supremacy of grace.
For such wisdom, vision, and sensitivity in relation to the law, we
offer great gratitude in the name of the One who obeyed the law in
the service of God and the redemption of humankind. Amen.

Listening

God of revelation:

Listening takes discipline, often more discipline than we possess. Not talking, though. Talking is easy. We always have a comment on most everything. Making noise is second nature to us.

Right now, however, we are talked out. Even if we were unaware of our need for listening, we desire to listen. We pray that in listening to you we will find some insight into the meaning and possibilities of what we hear and see around us.

God, we are disturbed as we listen to the sounds around us—
shrill sirens,
horns blown loudly by impatient people,
weather forecasts warning of impending disasters,
pleas for food coming from the shrunken faces of hungry
people,
boisterous talking among individuals seeking attention,
muffled sobs of grief,
silence, a thunderous silence that may be indicative of
growth or death.

We need to hear from you, O God, about all of that. And more.

Speak to us of how we should respond to the sounds of pain around us.

Speak to us about how we can experience grace.

Speak to us concerning the best ways to give public expression to the faith that we hold in private.

Speak to us about senseless illnesses and a proliferation of suffering. If there are not explanations, God, teach us to live with mystery and to be satisfied with the constancy of your presence.

Speak to us about death. How should we prepare for our own deaths? How can we find comfort when people close to us die? How are we to accept death as a temporal reality but not as an ultimate victory?

Speak to us about loneliness. Remind us that as long as you are God, we will never be alone.

Speak to us about worship and ministry. Save us from efforts to separate the two from each other and teach us how each is a part of the other.

O God, train the ears of our souls to hear even your slightest whisper. We are listening, God. We are listening to you, praying all the while that you are listening to us and readying yourself to speak to us again.

We pray through Jesus Christ, the perfect revelation of your hearing and speaking, your fleshed-out Word of redemptive response to our most basic human needs. Amen.

Love

O Perfect Love:

I bet sometimes you would just as soon we not talk about love at all as to go on and on speaking about it not knowing any more about the real nature of it than we do.

I confess confusion about love. I cannot always distinguish between love and sentimentality, love and nostalgia, love and an attraction to beauty, love and sex, love and feeling good. I need your instruction and guidance.

God, teach me about love, real love, your kind of love. Enable me to understand how love can be both

> tender and tough,
> vulnerable and strong,
> happy and sad,
> angry and empathetic,
> predictable and spontaneous,
> mature and childlike,
> outraged and forgiving,
> human and divine.

I want to understand love fully in order, with your help, to try to live by love faithfully.

At times, I need help loving myself. Somewhere I got the idea that to put myself down personally would exalt me spiritually. I get so aggravated with myself that I completely lose sight of the value you have instilled within me as you have within everyone else.

I defeat myself. I give up on myself. I refuse to forgive myself.

Correct me, God. Help me to know how to love myself appropriately in order to love beyond myself more satisfactorily.

At times I need help loving others. Prejudices get in my way. Jealousy stifles me. Selfishness threatens to destroy me and my relationships with people around me.

O God, teach me how to begin loving even those people whom I have trouble liking. Create within me a desire for the kind of fellowship with others in which love for one another continues to grow and unity with one another develops. Move me to love others more thoroughly in order that I may love you more truly.

At times I need help loving you. I don't understand why life is going as it is, and I get mad at you. I get confused about what I should do for myself and what I should expect you to do for me. I hold you responsible for experiences that defy any explanation at all, much less reasonable explanations.

O God, wipe out all the blind spots that keep me from seeing your eternally selfless, sacrificial love. Enable me to sustain an openness in my life that allows me to be infused by your love, served by your love, and strengthened by your love.

I know I have been created in your image. I am grateful for that. But I want more. I want my love to be patterned after your love. I want to be filled with a love that is born of faith, nurtured by hope, and always evidenced by expressions of grace.

Teach me about love, real love, your kind of love. Fill me with that love. Guide me in that love so that I can live by that love.

I pray in the name of Jesus, the embodiment of perfect love. Amen.

Lying

O God of truth:

Lying is a significant bother as well as a sin. One lie necessitates another and then another and then another. There is no end to it. Eventually every day is dominated by stringent and cautious efforts to support the lies of other days. If one lie is ever exposed, that's it; they all fall like dominoes.

I don't like to lie. I don't like people who lie. I think I would hate lying even if it wasn't wrong.

But I don't always tell the truth. I don't actually say anything untrue. I don't lie; I just

leave out certain parts of a story;

remain silent sometimes when I could speak;

don't tell all of the truth.

That does not qualify as lying, does it, God? That is all right, isn't it, God? My action literally does not fit the definition of lying. But morally, the principle . . . the principle of truth telling . . . the lifestyle of honesty . . . I see. I understand.

Please forgive me, God. And fill me with truth. I pray in the name of Truth incarnate. Amen.

Maundy Thursday

Redeeming God:

Today is a tough day.

Maundy Thursday brings us face-to-face with the Judas principle in our personal lives. In our world, too, love gets betrayed, loyalties fail, courage weakens, promises are broken. Not even the killing has ceased. We still have to have a Golgotha, an El Salvador, a Persian Gulf, a Serbia, or some other place where we can play havoc with the highest order of your creation.

Today is a tough day.

We seek a Gethsemane of sorts. We certainly desire to pray. We need forgiveness for our failures, our evil strategies, our slumber during the advent of tragedy, and our stake in the mass production of death.

Today is a tough day.

Toughest of all is what comes next. We seek to emulate the prayer of our Elder Brother and ask not for our wills to be done but for your will to be done. Not knowing exactly in what direction you may guide us or through what kind of revelation you may speak to us, we talk to you trembling like a fragile tent in an earthquake. For better or worse, though, we mean what we say: In our lives, let not our wills but your will be done.

There. We've said it.

Good God, enable us now to be up and going, whether our destination is a crucifixion or a resurrection—or by some divine act, both.

We pray in the name of the foot-washing, praying, saving Christ. Amen.

Mercy

Merciful God:
>Have mercy! Hear our cries for mercy—
>>the loud audible ones screamed in desperation,
>>the soft-spoken ones offered in the liturgy of a
>>worshiping congregation,
>>the whispered ones that spring from our meditation,
>>and the silent ones that are muffled by a shame that
>>fears confession.
>
>Have mercy on us, O God—
>>that we may not be helpless in the face of temptation,
>>that we may not be locked up in stifling guilt,
>>that we may find meaning in our labor,
>>that we may know community among our friends,
>>that we may find joy and peace both inside and outside
>>ourselves.
>
>Have mercy on us, O God. And make us merciful. Enable us to
>give to others freely that which we request from you so passionately.
>God, make us merciful so that
>>mistakes can be excused and requests for forgiveness
>>granted,
>>needs around us may strike compassion within us and evoke
>>ministry from us,
>>prejudices may be eradicated and grudges removed,
>>all people may be saved from hunger, assured of justice,
>>and encouraged toward peace.
>
>Grant mercy to us, merciful God.
>God, you are mercy. Make us your merciful children.
>Believing that you not only hear our prayers but respond to our
>requests, confidently we turn from somber pleas for your mercy to
>joyful adoration of your merciful nature; through Jesus Christ who
>taught us what mercy looks like and what joy feels like. Amen.

Missions

O God, Light to the nations:
  We find it a pleasure to talk to you about missions rather than have you talk to us. Please hear our voices and listen without speaking.
  Hear first our offering of thanks for people who serve you around the world—for people who spend a lifetime away from family members and familiar places in order to speak and work on behalf of the gospel. Hear us, God. Listen to our voices and please don't tell us more about our mission right now.
  Hear now our confessions, O God.
>   In our days of prayer for missions we have found more
>   delight in the fellowship of the days than in the
>   responsibility of prayer.
>   In our missions offerings we have discovered how to make
>   gifts of financial support substitutes for personal
>   involvement.
>   In our missions studies we have opted for inspiration
>   over challenge and preferred increased knowledge about
>   missions over enhanced participation in missions.
>   We have prayed for the call to missions to come to
>   others, but we have insulated our own sensitivities from
>   that summons.
>   We have asked for specific jobs to be done by others,
>   but we have hedged in making available ourselves, our
>   family members, or even our friends.
>   We have prayed for venturesome boldness but enjoyed the
>   smugness of what we already know, feel, and do.
>   Forgive us, O God.
  Hear also our intercessions, God.
>   Strengthen those who speak the Word of God courageously
>   in hostile cultures.
>   Enlighten those who translate Scriptures in order that
>   all people can read of truth.
>   Enrich those who teach basic skills in order that people
>   can grow, work, and serve.
>   Guide those who provide medical services for all kinds
>   of sicknesses.
>   Sustain those who distribute food to the hungry and
>   offer instruction in food production.

Hear us, O God. Please just listen to our voices and refrain from talking to us about our mission as we are praying.

Now come words of praise, God.

>You hear our confessions and forgive.
>
>You listen to our intercessions and strengthen.
>
>You bless us with a message of Good News and a ministry of reconciliation.
>
>You promise that the Christ whom we proclaim will be the Christ who ultimately reigns.

All praise be to you, sovereign God, who taught us about missions through the revelation of your redemptive mission to us in Jesus Christ.

Before we cease to pray, O God, we need to tell you that we can still hear your voice. You are continuing to talk to us. Have we not said enough or done enough? We have promised to pray, to give, and to support missions. We have pledged our love for missions and offered praise and thanksgiving for missions. Why do you continue to speak? What do you want from us?

Everything or nothing at all?

The entirety of our lives?

Personal involvement in missions?

How can you expect so much? Why such a desire for total commitment? What right do you have—— Oh, my goodness. Sure, I know. I see. My salvation comes from your mission in which nothing was held back and everything was given.

Thanks be to you, God of missions. Here is my life offered as is this prayer, through Jesus Christ my Lord. Amen.

Monday

God of time and eternity:

Mondays are so long. From here the remainder of the week seems to stretch out interminably. Unlike Sunday, nothing about Monday appears very holy.

Choirs have been replaced by customers.

The printed order of worship has been set aside for duplicated work orders.

The majestic sounds of the pipe organ have given way to annoying rings of a telephone.

The Bible has taken second place to sales reports.

Fellowship in a congregation has been replaced by competition among office staff members.

Monday is not a holy day. Not by a long shot.

But we cannot ignore a faint hint of praise. At the deepest level of our existence, with thoughts sharp and wills in touch with our commitments, we discern the true nature of all days, Mondays included. And we give you thanks for this day of life, its opportunities for service, and its potential for meaning.

No day is holy apart from you, not even a Sunday. When you are present, though, every day is holy, even a Monday. In your presence labor can become a prayer, a towel can become an article of ministry, and a common conversation can yield a word from eternity.

O God, please join us today. Or to pray more honestly, O God, grant us the wisdom to join you, today and every day.

Thank you, God, for the good gift of Monday, a holy day. We offer our thanks through Jesus Christ who was and is Lord of Monday even as of the sabbath. Amen.

Music

God of all good gifts, Source of all true inspiration:

From the moment we first learned to force air through our lips enough to call it whistling or to blow steadily into empty bottles causing a sound with some kinship to song, to our first special thrill generated by the genius of a symphony or the glory of a choir singing "Hallelujah," we sensed that music must come from you. Now we know.

Thank you, God, for the gift of music and for the inspiration that
causes it to be written and performed.
>You have provided for us a near-perfect vehicle for the
expression of our most profound emotions.
You have given us reasons for music, instruments for music,
voices for music, and words for music.
The inspiration of your Holy Spirit perpetually prods a
vision of you as the Divine Musician.
O God of music, we need this special gift.
Sometimes life is like an eighth note: events occur
quickly, joyously, memorably.
At other times we need a whole note to hold at length
our ideas, exclamations, and commitments.
Just as there is music for battle, there is music for peace.
From the same instrument can come funeral dirges and
celebrations of life.
We need it all.
O Musician God, please do not ever stop giving. Keep on inspiring people sensitive to the rhythms of life and the direction of your
will to keep on providing music that gives to us all
the relief of expression,
the joy of elation,
the nurture of confession,
the strength of devotion.
We pledge to be good stewards of the music you have entrusted to
us. Nurture your people to live as a choir filled with individuals
whose minds, hearts, and actions, as well as mouths, sing praise and
glory to your holy name.
We pray in the name of the Music Maker, Jesus Christ. Amen.

Nation

God of all nations:
We pray for our nation, following the instructions of your Word.
As we do, please prevent the formation within us of an uncritical
equating of love for the nation and devotion to you. Keep our loyalty
to this land forever subordinate to our allegiance to the lordship of
Christ. Enable us to maintain the moral superiority of our service to
you over our participation in government.

With profound gratitude we express thanksgiving for our nation—
    for the heritage we celebrate and formative ideas that
        continue to inspire,
    for the freedom we enjoy and the commitment to freedom
        that makes us responsible,
    for lofty vision of purpose and government processes
        open to citizens' involvement.

With humility and sincerity we seek forgiveness for our failure as a nation. Our past is marked by sin as well as success. At times we have
    enslaved people,
    denied individual rights,
    magnified our will rather than your will,
    and lent support to wrong rather than vigorously working
        for right.

Forgive us, O God. Forgive us and
    never let us give up on the intention of good
        government;
    never let us lose sight of the dignity and rights of
        every citizen;
    never allow us to attempt to isolate ourselves from the
        other nations of the earth;
    never allow our passion for freedom to weaken in
        intensity or narrow in scope;
    never permit us to discourage dreamers or to discharge
        pioneers who desire to lead us toward a better way.

With sympathetic understanding, we pray for our leaders.
    Grant to the president the conscience you intend for the
        chief political officer of any nation.
    Instill wisdom within the members of the Senate and the
        House of Representatives.
    Bestow upon the justices of the Supreme Court sensitive
        skills in legal interpretation.
    Enable military officials to envision nonmilitary
        responses as viable options in solving critical problems.

With a commitment to faithful citizenship, we pray for the people of the nation—ourselves.
    Teach us to translate personal convictions into political
        actions.
    Deliver us from the tendency to depend upon government

for that which we can rightly do for ourselves.

Grant us the ability to separate truth from propaganda.

Silence our nonconstructive criticisms and enable us to
face crises responsibly rather than to seek scapegoats
fanatically.

Instruct us regarding the difference between the necessity
of political compromise and the repugnance of moral
compromise.

Strengthen our commitment to the guarantee of justice as
the minimal standard in all human relationships.

With a desire for ethical integrity, we pray for the influence of our
nation within the family of nations.

Broaden our patriotism that it may be inclusive rather
than exclusive.

Establish as our distinctives not the brandishing of
power but the practice of compassion.

Inspire us so that we will always be the first to speak
out in the condemnation of prejudice and injustice as we
seek equality among the citizenry.

Shape us into a model of peacemaking.

Grant that our greatest contributions to the people of the world
may reside in the realm of the spirit.

O God, we know the nation is not the church. We understand that
ultimate loyalty belongs to your sovereignty alone. And so we pray
for our nation in the name of the One who taught us to give to Caesar
what is Caesar's but never to give to Caesar that which belongs only
to you. Amen.

New Year

God of the ages:

A new year has dawned, and some of us are not ready to let loose
of the old one. Looking back over the past twelve months, we see a
time of new births, marriages, graduations, promotions, and victories.
The advent of a new year indicates that it is time for us to care for all
that has been celebrated, to work on that which has been enjoyed, to
handle responsibly that which up until now has been a novelty. A
new year appears as a threat—a stretch of time that represents a more
difficult period of life.

God of the future:

A new year has dawned, and others of us could not be happier. We are ready for the past year to be over, hoping that its conclusion means a termination of the difficulties experienced in it—failures, losses, relocation, broken covenants, deaths, violence, bitterness, and worries. The advent of a new year signals a renewal of hope.

God of the present:

No one prayer can suffice for a whole year or even an entire day. So here is the first prayer of many to be offered during this new year. O God, during these next twelve months,

enable us to walk by faith as well as by sight;
strengthen us that we might reject the seduction of
   temptation;
deliver us from making the same old mistakes again;
prod us to grow in our knowledge of the Scriptures;
instruct us as we establish life-enhancing priorities;
prohibit us from becoming too narrow in either our
   relationships or our beliefs;
enlighten us regarding the general nature of your will
   as well as your specific intentions for our lives.

As we journey through this uncharted stretch of new time, guide us, God. Guide us that we may worship only the One worthy of worship, that we may follow as Lord only the One who is the Christ.

Guiding God,

Open our eyes that we may always see you.
Open our minds that we may think on your truths.
Open our hearts that we may love you.
Open our mouths that we may share your Good News.
Open our hands that we may give to you and serve others in
   your name.

At the dawn of this new year, O God, we strengthen our grip on your promises, renew our determination to live in your love, and commit ourselves to follow you leadership in faithful obedience.

We pray in the name of the Pioneer. Amen.

Offerings

Great Giving God:

Often it occurs to us how much better corporate worship could be if it were just "spiritual." Prayers that set before us our sins, Scriptures that bring to mind our human dilemmas, and offerings that cause us to think of money tend to get our attention diverted from the "spiritual."

We will deal with our sins on our own. We will seek ways out of difficult situations with a little help from our friends. We will speak with our bankers and brokers about money. We would like to keep our relationship with you unmarred by such material concerns.

But, of course, corporate worship cannot take place that way. Indeed, you care about all of life—the spiritual and the physical, the good and the bad.

So, as an act of worship we make offerings to you of our resources—our money, our time, our abilities, and our plans.

God, here are our lives! Accept us as you do other offerings and use us in

the spreading of your Word,
the doing of your will, and
the coming of your kingdom.

O God, here are our lives!

We pray in the name of your incomprehensible offering to us, your Son, Jesus Christ. Amen.

Patience

O God of endless mercy:
    Patience is something I have precious little of, and what little I
have is almost gone.
>   I am more than a little weary of the way things are going
>   in this world.
>   I am fed up with religionists whose message is self-serving,
>   whose goal is power, and whose actions are immoral.
>   I have had enough of the dictators abroad and the
>   evangelists at home who see no good in anything that they
>   did not plan and who speak only destructive, never
>   redemptive, words.
>   I have had about all I can take of uncalled-for suffering
>   and the deaths of innocent people whether in the desert
>   places of the Middle East or the stark white rooms of a
>   hospital in my hometown.
>   I am worn out by broken promises, fractured relationships,
>   betrayed trusts, and frantic attempts to hold things together
>   in the wake of all of that.

    I'm sure I don't have to tell you all of this. You know me. My
patience wears thin. Suddenly I want to scream at someone, to find a
scapegoat, to hit somebody, to eradicate a whole way of life so that it
will no longer be available to those who desire it. I need help—the
kind of help that only you can give.
>   Work on my patience with me, O God. Strengthen what little I
>   have. Grant me more.
>   Deliver me from the kind of actions that make me look like
>   someone who has never known you or served you.
>   Prevent me from losing, or being lost to, the distinctive
>   character traits born of Christian faith, hope, and love.
>   Save me from doing in one moment of extreme passion or
>   absolute desperation that which will alter adversely all
>   future moments.

    I need more patience, God. I am trying to exercise the patience I
have, but I need more. Please help me.
    And please, O God, do not lose your patience with me.
    My restless prayer is formed in the name of the peace-giving
Christ. Amen.

Peace

O God of peace:

We pray for peace. Is it a waste of time? Is peace possible?

As a hymn writer has so well expressed: "Come, peace of God, and dwell again on earth!. . .Come, peace of God, and rule within our hearts!"[1] Yes, God. Please.

"Come, peace of God, and dwell again on earth!"

Prejudice prevails.

Arguments aggravate.

Jealousies jaundice.

Doubts destroy.

Conflict consumes.

Suspicions suffocate.

Wars kill.

"Come, peace of God, and rule within our hearts!" Yes again, God. Please.

We are pessimistic, if not fatalistic, about peace. So much can go wrong, and does. So many problems persist. Just when we think all is going well, something goes wrong, very wrong, and we mutter that we knew it would happen that way.

As we repeat the lines, we recognize their interrelatedness as well as their distinctions. We request peace within and without, in our hearts and throughout the earth. But we can't quite shake the questions. Great God, is such peace possible? Can it happen? Do any assurances exist?

Teach us of peace. Turn our faces toward the Prince of Peace. Enable us to see how he brought peace—

peace to fractured personalities,

peace to demented, tormented minds,

peace to a lake wind-whipped into a churning frenzy,

peace to emotions gone berserk.

Of course, that One was, and is, your Son. You have been about peacemaking as long as you have been about world making and person shaping.

You spoke of peace amid thunder.

You told of peace from within a whirlwind.

[1]From "Come, Peace of God, and Dwell Again on Earth," by May Rowland (1928).

You brought peace to frantic persons roaming a wilderness.

You made peace possible by means of a violent, warlike crucifixion.

Good God, it can happen! Peace is possible. Assurances appear throughout your work and your Word.

Come, peace of God, and dwell again on earth.

Come, peace of God, and rule within our hearts.

We ask for peace.

And we ask in the name of the One whose life has the potential to function as a sword but whose life was given that all people might know peace, Jesus the crucified-in-conflict, resurrected-in-peace Lord. Amen.

Praise

God of creation and redemption, Divine Creator, Compassionate Redeemer:

Even before we knew we *could* praise you, we felt we *should* praise you. We have seen your work in our world. We have experienced your presence in our lives.

We praise you gratefully, O God. We have received bountifully from your goodness—

a creation that satisfies us as well as sustains us—
we praise you, O God;

relationships that enrich us as well as challenge us—
we praise you, O God;

ideas that enlighten us as well as guide us—
we praise you, O God;

music that sets our souls to soaring as well as our lips to singing—
we praise you, O God.

redemption that fills us with joy as well as cleanses us of sin—
we praise you, O God.

We have received bountifully from your goodness. We praise you gratefully. Our constant desire is to offer unceasing praise to you, O God. We want to praise you

when times are bad and good,

when health is poor and sound,

when faith is weak and strong,

when life is empty and full.

Accept our praise, God. you are the One whom we adore, whom we worship, whom we seek to serve, and to whom we pray.

We praise you

with our words, thoughts, and actions;

with our lips, hands, and feet;

with our hymns, prayers, and offerings.

We praise you, O God, through Jesus Christ who embodied as well as evoked praise. Amen.

Prayer

O God, who invites our attention and delights in our devotion:
    We feel more than a little awkward about this admission, God, but we are going through with it because we need divine direction. Sometimes we don't know when to pray or what to pray about. Frequently we catch ourselves asking you for guidance or making requests in relation to matters that we are not sure qualify as suitable subjects for prayer.
    Though in no way do we imagine ourselves capable of understanding your thoughts and ways, as a result of your past revelations, we do hold some convictions about the nature of your interests.
    We don't think you care who wins a Little League baseball
        game, or for that matter, the Super Bowl.
    We see no divine significance in whether our families buy
        and drive a General Motors car or an American Motors auto.
Please do not think us presumptuous or irreligious, God.
    We hear people talking about their prayers for
        divine assistance in deciding between the purchase of a
            yellow chair or a red one,
        an exertion of divine influence to guarantee a campus
            sorority's acceptance of their daughter,
        their favorite football team to go through the
            season undefeated,
        the recovery of an injured pet.
Truthfully, we are angered rather than impressed or inspired by such talk. Knowing of your interest in and the importance of prayers for
        the peaceable defusing of the political powder keg in the
            Middle East,
        the care of starving people in the drought-plagued regions
            of Africa,
        the insights of laboratory scientists seeking cures for cancer,
            AIDS, and heart diseases,
        the evangelization of scores of virtually pagan persons,
we cannot bring ourselves to bother you with requests for help in fixing a flat tire, selecting a wall painting, holing a long putt on the golf course, or buying a new suit.
    If we need a reprimand and correction, please administer both quickly and convincingly. Otherwise, help us better to use our minds and energies in the manner you intend so that we will not be asking

you about concerns we should be able to handle on our own. Enable us to see when it is more religious just to take action than to pray about what to do.

At the same time, please know how thankful we are for the endless patience and sensitive concern you demonstrate when listening to us talk with you about some of our concerns that never should have been made the subjects of prayers.

We speak in the name of the One who taught us how to pray. Amen.

Questions

Responsive God of revelation:

Most of our prayers are fed by mixed feelings and perplexing confusion as well as unrelenting commitment. This one is no exception.

Questions are as much a part of our lives as answers. Some inquiries hound us constantly. Others come and go with varying degrees of intensity. Some questions provoke thought processes that are fun. Others, especially the ones that never seem to get answered, pick at us, burn in us, and rub us raw spiritually.

O God, we want to set before you some of the questions that trouble us most. In doing so, we mean no disrespect whatsoever. Our sole reason for pursuing answers to these questions is to embrace new convictions while strengthening old ones. Please hear us, and respond as you will.

Is good to be recognized only against a backdrop of evil?

Can angels sing even when it is raining?

Must troubles, sickness, and death continue even at Christmas?

Do innocent people have to expect that they will forever be victimized by events they did not instigate and worry they did not cause?

Why are so many folks fearful of freedom?

Can faith exist without nagging doubts?

How is it that my community can get so excited about the blessings of your Son's birth and be so oblivious to the responsibilities related to it?

Must Jesus always show up in our midst in a manger or

riding on a donkey?

Why can spring, with its budding flowers and greening
grass, not arrive apart from killer tornadoes?

Will we ever be able to enjoy a parade of celebration
without the tormenting fear of betrayal or assassination?

Is there any way to get to Easter without confronting
crucifixion?

Well, enough of the questions. Sometimes we grow weary of
asking them, wishful of forgetting them. But there are times, many
times actually, when we suspect that you are the One who plants the
questions in our minds and encourages our wrestling matches with
them.

Pondering the questions that nag us prompts thoughts about some
of the convictions that give us peace. God, we are thankful for
unshakable certainties:

Good news is available to people everywhere.

Joy can withstand misfortune.

Divine promises are fulfilled.

Crises pass.

Hurt fades.

Real freedom cannot be destroyed by iron bars or armed
guards.

Doubts can prod a discovery of faith.

Strong winds are finally stilled.

Cynical despair gives way to biblical hope.

Life can overcome death.

We can see you as a baby in a manger, as the Savior on a cross, as
the resurrected Christ by an empty tomb, as the living, reigning Lord.

Thank you, God, for taking us seriously, graciously receiving our
questions, and lovingly nurturing our convictions.

We pray, whether raising questions or declaring certainties, in the
name of the One who raised almost as many questions as he asserted
absolutes. Amen.

Quiet

God of sight and sound, blindness and quietness:

All is quiet right now, and we are not real sure we like it. We are
accustomed to noises—noises that confuse thoughts and make a
discovery of meaning difficult. Sounds besiege our eardrums and stir
up storms in our souls:

> music channeled into office suites to provide a poor cover-up for
> the jangling of phones and clattering of typewriters;
> bells ringing, signaling for us when to work, when to eat,
> when to answer a call, when to stop for the day;
> televisions and radios blaring entertainment that does not
> entertain, advertisements that equate self-worth with
> material possessions, and news reports that cause a disturbance;
> people talking incessantly—not really communicating, but
> talking—complaining about the weather, speculating about
> politics, asking "how are you?" but not really wanting to know.

Why are we so fearful of an absence of noise? Are we afraid to
hear our heartbeat, to sense the direction of our surging emotions, to
listen to the dialogue between our minds and our bodies? Or are we
scared that we may hear screams for help within our world, coupled
with the whispers of your will summoning us to action?

O God, please preserve moments of quietness that we may hear
from without and within the sounds that cause us to confront reality
and to move toward profound spiritual commitment:

> cries of a newborn baby ready to be fed and loved;
> sobs of someone who has just lost a companion by death and
> needs comfort for grief;
> shouts of persons protesting some social evil;
> promptings from the Holy Spirit;
> begging pleas for help from starving people;
> thoughts from a person who just discovered joy;
> words whispered by Holy Scripture;
> anthems of a church choir.

O God, send a hush in our midst. Create stillness in our souls.
Make the quietness that comes from the ministry of your Spirit so
much a part of our experience that even amid a cacophony of clang-
ing, banging, bombast, and booms within our society we may know
the fullness of a redemptive quietness in which you speak to us in a
still small voice and in our hearing we realize re-creation.

We pray in the name of the One who could convey more meaning in a moment of silence than others can communicate in hours of talk. Amen.

Race

God of all nations and people:

Looking around us, we see people with different colors of skin. Is that bad or good? Should we notice skin color?

For a while we prayed for you to make us oblivious to the color of a person's skin. Now, though, color seems important. We sense that we should be aware of, take seriously, and respect an individual's race.

Well, right or wrong, the pigmentation (or lack of it) in people's skin is an object of our attention.

Our first response to that recognition is thanksgiving. We express gratitude to you for including individual distinctions within creation.

But then, God, we are seized by an oppressive guilt. We recognize our complicity in a history and society filled with prejudice, discrimination, segregation, and depersonalization on the basis of the color of people's skin. Great God, forgive us.

Right now, racial differences create tensions, foment misunderstandings, and threaten violence throughout the communities of our global village. Call out from among us persons whom you will strengthen and use as

facilitators of understanding,

bridges of reconciliation, and

shapers of peace.

O God, we pray for a future that embraces a recognition of similarities, a commitment to equality, and evidences of mutual respect among all persons that are as strong as the differences, hatred, and attacks on one another that have marked our past. Teach us how to live together in harmony. More importantly, help us to love one another.

Instill within us a vision of the human family that motivates us, all of us—regardless of skin color—to live as brothers and sisters seeking to please our Creator.

We pray in the name of our dark-skinned Elder Brother who spent his entire life trying to tear down all the barriers that separate people from one another and from you. Amen.

Redemption

God of redemption:
  Redeem your creation! We have
    taken it for granted,
    polluted it,
    exploited it,
    desecrated it,
    bombed it.
  Redeem our world!
    We are torn.
    We are confused.
    We are mixed up on priorities. Right now, our attention
      shuffles back and forth between a summit conference of
      world leaders, a National Football League game in Miami,
      and the itinerary for a business trip to San Francisco.
    We can't focus on what is wrong long enough even to
      work hard to get it fixed.
  Redeem the church! All too often our church is just like any other
organization
    counting its money,
    totaling its membership,
    contacting prospects,
    drawing up salable programs, and
    carrying on business as usual.
  Redeem our lives!
    Through forgiveness, deal with our sins.
    By means of a new vision, address our lostness.
    With meaning, speak to our search for fulfillment.
    In Christ, confront our commitment.
  In creation, in the world, in the church, and in our lives, may your
kingdom come and your will be done. Redeem us completely that all
the redeemed may act like it as well as say so.
  Redeem us through the Redeemer, in whose name we request
redemption and through whose ministry we expect to find it. Amen.

Renewal

O God, whose Holy Spirit brings life:
> Sometimes we just seem to run down—to wear out spiritually.
> Faith demands more energy than we have.
> Prayers in search of the divine will are set aside for the more
> expedient exercise of our own wills.
> Hope fades significantly, beaten down by one stark reality
> after another in which evil has been victorious.
> Love requires that we give far more than we want to give.
> Worship is more a routine of the human community than a
> route into the divine presence.
> We need renewal. We need freshening up. We need spiritual oases

from which to drink in order to enliven our parched spirits on
pilgrimage.

> We pray for renewal in the church.
>> Where mediocrity has become acceptable, make us
>> uncomfortable until we serve you with nothing other
>> than our best.
>> Where familiarity with the gospel has dulled our
>> attentiveness to the proclamation of it, awaken us again
>> to its power and importance.
>> Where enjoyment amid fellowships of believers has bred
>> unconcern about new converts, remind us of the
>> necessity of extending invitations in the sharing of our
>> faith.
>> Where success in ministries of the past has lulled us
>> into apathy about ministries needed in the present, shake
>> our spirits until we are alert.
>> Where stewardship of finances has been substituted for a
>> stewardship of all life, challenge us until we change.
> We pray for the church, O God. Renew the church, O Lord.

> We pray for renewal in ourselves.
>> Where a distant commitment to Jesus Christ has been made
>> to suffice for growth in Christlikeness, renew us.
>> Where forgiveness has been a doctrine believed but not a
>> spirit demonstrated and a matter of the will exercised,
>> renew us.

Where prayer has been affirmed more than practiced,
revitalize us.
Where compassion has desired grace for ourselves but not
extended grace to others, encourage us.
Where sharing the gospel has become a professional
responsibility rather than each individual's joy, help us.
We pray for ourselves, O God. Renew us, O Lord.

It has been dry a long time for many of us. Come, Lord Jesus.
Come into the fellowship of the church. Come into our discipleship.
Renew us and bless us that we may become agents of renewal and
blessings to others; in the name of the One who can make all things
new. Amen.

Rest

Great God of the sabbath:
Years before our time, Augustine prayed that you would make
people restless until they found their rest in you. What a wonderful
prayer!
Augustine's words are applicable for us. We cannot improve on
his request or harbor any greater aspiration for our lives.
God, make us restless until we find our rest in you.
We pray in the name of the One who as Lord of the sabbath made
rest a part of salvation. Amen.

Resurrection

God of creation, compassion, crucifixion, resurrection, and redemption:

Sometimes we have trouble getting up in the morning because of the difficulties of the preceding evening. How difficult it is for us to conceive of our brother Jesus getting up from the dead!

Besides, resurrections seem foreign to our world. What we know best are

> broken promises,
> frayed relationships,
> aborted dreams,
> sorrowful deaths.

We have grown accustomed to narratives without happy endings, rejoicing that takes place despite tragedy, and incidents that make no sense and bear no promise. When it comes to resurrections, we are borderline cynics.

We don't like it this way, God, but frankly, most days we are not real sure there is another way. That is why the resurrection of Jesus catches us off guard. He comes to us early in the morning, late in the evening, in a garden, beside the expressway, or at the office, and we don't recognize him. We call him by the wrong name. We are not accustomed to resurrections.

Please do not hear us as complaining, though. We are as profoundly thankful for the resurrection of Jesus as we are surprised by it. We take hope that reversals, major reversals, are possible.

Stretch our faith and enlarge our hope to the point that we can fully embrace the resurrected Lord. By the power with which you raised Jesus from death, raise within us courage, integrity, dreams, goals, plans, joy, forgiveness, grace, faith, and peace that we may know life. Enable us to follow the risen Christ as well as greet him and to experience

> promises kept,
> relationships restored,
> dreams realized,
> death that gives way to life.

God of resurrection, send the raised-up Lord to live within us in order that we may live with you—forever. Amen.

Reverence

Most Holy God:

Even as we begin to address you in prayer, we are aware that many of our predecessors in faith refused to speak your name for fear of irreverence. We identify with that spirit if not with that practice.

Certainly we approach your presence with wonder and awe. To ponder titles for you is to be cognizant of your divinity and our humanity—Yahweh, Elohim, El Shaddai, Jehovah, Creator, Redeemer, Father of mercies, Light of lights, King of kings, Lord of lords. For us, speaking your name is in no way an act of irreverence; rather it is an honest attempt at much-needed communion. To be sure, we know the reality of humility, but we long for the possibility of fellowship with you.

Oh, sometimes we forget—forget our finitude, forget your divinity. We lose sight of the biblical truth that your thoughts are not our thoughts and your ways are not our ways. Forgive us, O God. Forgive us

> when we attempt to reduce you to a manageable size and thus see you as too small;
>
> when we sense a need to justify your actions with our rationalizations and think we can explain your nature completely;
>
> when we restlessly wish to rely upon you by sight rather than to trust you in faith;
>
> when we carelessly attach your authority to our selfish plans in order to gain credibility.

Form within us thoughts that challenge our smugness and presumptuousness in relation to you.

You are mystery—immortal, invisible, all-wise.

You are perfect love—ever self-giving, author of our living.

You are grace—initiator of acceptance for the unacceptable.

We reverence you, O God, in mind and body, with words and deeds, through belief and behavior, knowing that the most profound expressions of reverence are to be found in devotion and obedience.

We pray in Christ's name, the One who helped us understand best how intimate love and awesome reverence are united in authentic commitment. Amen.

Scripture Reading

God of the Bible:

Poised to read your Word once again, we request your assistance.
Help us to hear, O God,
to hear the pathos of the writers' life situations,
to hear the passion of the writers' desire for
communication,
to hear the enthusiasm of the writers' faith convictions.
Help us to see, O God,
to see the dimensions of the dilemma faced by our
predecessors in faith,
to see the implications for our discipleship displayed
in the lifestyle of those first disciples,
to see the transformation that is made possible when
Christ is Lord.
Help us to understand, O God,
to understand how a writer's words addressed to people
in another day constitute your Word to us today,
to understand the meaning and message of Scripture for
the multifaceted sweep of our lives,
to understand the faith, hope, and love that can enter
us, dwell within us, and enable us to live with faith,
hope, and love.
As we read the Scriptures, God,
keep us from flinching, turning away, and thus failing
to encounter your Word,
keep us from blinking, closing our minds, and thus failing
to see your truth,
keep us from hiding behind any excuse that will prevent
us from being engaged by your Spirit.

Pervade our reading of the Bible with your presence. If the
message seems strange and some words are unfamiliar to us, encourage us to keep on reading. And listening. Help us to discover all your
Word and to incorporate it into all of our lives.

In the name of the Word above all other words, we offer these
words. Amen.

Sex

Great Creator God:

As we begin to speak with you about sex, we must admit reticence. Words do not form easily for this prayer. A bit of discomfort gives us cause for hesitation.

At times we have been led to believe that the subject of sex is best treated when left unaddressed. At the other extreme, though, we have witnessed a virtual obsession with discussions of sex. While we are not satisfied with silence on this matter, we are aware that unfortunately the vocabulary related to sexual concerns, like the primal meaning of sexual activity, has been cheapened critically by crude secularists. Thus, we pray first for wisdom to know how to pray at all about this important aspect of life. Save us from both the irresponsibility of silence on sex and the perversity of an idolatry of sex.

We will start with thanksgiving. Sex was your idea. Sexual distinctions between men and women are the result of your creation. You declared that reality to be good. We agree. In your infinite wisdom you provided for a pleasurable act of sexual union between a man and a woman to aid in the realization of the wonder of intimacy and to exist as the means by which human beings can join you in the ongoing creation of new persons. Thank you, God, for the richness you have brought to our lives through your good gifts of masculinity and femininity and thus the possibility of a one-flesh relationship in covenant love.

Confession is a difficulty every bit as much as a necessity. We need forgiveness for sexual sins—

for using sex to attain social acceptance and to achieve
personal goals,
for selling sex like just another marketable commodity,
for reducing sex to the status of a glandular need to be
satisfied,
for manipulating sex in the interest of public advertising,
for separating sex from a marital fidelity forged out of
commitments and love.

What we have done is almost inexcusable—

pandering sexually explicit materials for the purpose of
titillation,
trading sexual favors for economic gain,
prostituting personal dignity in the production of pornography,

establishing a performance of the mechanics of sex as
the criterion for determining the quality of a relationship.
Please forgive us, O God.

We turn to intercession next, O God. We pray for individuals who
are the victims of rampant sexual passions—

for a child sexually abused by an unconscionable adult,

for a woman who has been violated by the hideous crime
of rape,

for a young boy whose future health has been risked
because of the damage perpetrated by published
obscenities,

for a young girl who has sacrificed her dignity in a
desperate pursuit of popularity,

for a wife who has been emotionally devastated by an
insensitive husband who uses her as an impersonal
receptacle for sexual relief rather than loves her as a
marital mate of dignity and worth,

for a man who foolishly assumes that the litmus test of
his masculinity is performance-based sexual
promiscuity,

for a society that seems to have lost its way amid a
morass of sexual immorality.

Dedication is decisive. With love we devote ourselves to service
as instruments for the implementation of your divine will. In obedience we will defend human decency. With conviction we will protest
obscenity. With grace we will forgive those guilty of sexual sins.
With pleasure we will claim all your purposes for sexuality.

Please accept our grateful affirmation of your intention in creation
that sex be seen as good; our determined resolution to know the joy,
intimacy, and potential of sexual union only within the commitments
of covenant love; and our dedication to remain open and responsive
to your leadership in this as in all other areas of life.

We pray in the name of the fully human One who freed persons to
live as the males and females you created us to be. Amen.

Sleep

God of Jacob and all other sleepers, dreamers, dream makers, and dream interpreters:

As children, we learned to kneel beside our beds and say something like, "Now I lay me down to sleep. I pray thee, God, my soul to keep. If I should die before I wake, I pray thee, God, my soul to take." Although sometimes it was a perfunctory act with a mere repetition of words, we did pray as a postlude to the day and a prelude to sleep.

Forgive us now, O God, when we fail to bend either knee or soul to you, when we remain silent before you concerning the events of the day, and when we take health-giving sleep for granted. Make us ever conscious of our need to pray—to be in communion with you—at both the beginning and the ending of every day.

Childhood-memorized assertions offered as prayer have become adult-contemplated pleas in prayer.

Strengthen us spiritually so prior promises kept give us the confidence that nurtures security, and so no anxiety about tomorrow prevents relaxation tonight.

Spare us the kind of demonic behavior that spawns bad dreams that disturb our souls and cause our bodies to toss and turn.

Increase our faith so that we trust ourselves to you completely, whether asleep or awake, believing that we are in your care whether living or dead.

We speak to you in the name of the One who gives us the serenity to close our eyes and sets before us a ministry that makes both sleeping and waking meaningful. Amen.

Social Justice

God of the Exodus, source of the only power that eradicates
prejudice, and inspirer of peace:

We give you thanks for the vision of a just society passed along to
us by your prophets in every generation. Some heard it as a com-
mandment. Others found it to be a source of judgment. A few saw it
as a divinely given dream. We gratefully accept the vision as all of
that. And more.

Honestly though, God, the immensity of the challenges before us
weakens the intensity of our gratitude. At present, the vision of a just
society creates a heavy burden.

The need for liberation increases faster than ministries of
liberation can be formed.

Violence continues to command a vigorous loyalty among
persons bent on using it to reorder society.

Poverty remains a cancerous blight eating away at
individual dignity and communal order.

Injustice persists as a nemesis to liberty.

Nevertheless, we rededicate ourselves to implementing the
redemptive dream.

If prejudice must exist, prejudice us toward a pursuit of
equality.

If bias must continue, bias us in favor of the oppressed.

If unrest must persist, disturb our souls until we work for
peace with our lives.

If hatred must find expression, teach us to hate systemic
bigotry, institutional racism, and any national policy of
apartheid.

If anger must bother us, make us angry at injustice, angry
enough to serve as advocates for justice.

We give ourselves anew to the realization of the holy vision, not
only praying for but working for

nations made strong by their commitment to justice, not
by their stockpiles of destructive weapons;

communities shaped by the force of reconciling love, not
by the power of competing factions;

and people judged by their character, not by the color of
their skin.

Use us, O God. Use us

to find homes for the homeless,
to offer bread to the hungry,
to eradicate structures of prejudice,
to tear down barriers of discrimination,
to construct avenues of understanding,
to facilitate reconciliation,
to bring peaceful solidarity to our global family.

O God, hear our pleas for help in battling injustice. Accept our dedication to the dream of equality and peace that you inspired. And bless us with strength and perseverance as we seek to build a society in which justice exists as a stable reality and grace as an occasional surprise.

We pray and work to cooperate with you in implementing answers to our prayers in the name of the redeemer-liberator, Jesus the Christ. Amen.

Specifics

God of the Incarnation in a specific time and place:

If we could always pray to you in generalities, prayer would not be such a bother. You know the language we have in mind: thank you for everything we have received, forgive our sins, help all people who need you, and lead us. The generalities are familiar. And rather easy.

But Jesus taught us to be specific—very specific. So we will attempt to pray in specifics.

We offer thanks to you, O God. Thanks for beauty, brilliant blue skies, warm sunshine, multicolored flowers, all shades of green. Hear our gratitude for meaningful conversations with friends, quiet meals that bond relationships as well as bring pleasure, sensitive words of affirmation, helpful phone calls that come at just the right moments, picnics that feed the soul as well as the stomach. Thank you, God, for chocolate candy, pizza, hamburgers, ice cream, spaghetti, and fresh spring berries.

With much more difficulty we include specifics in our requests for forgiveness. O God, we ask for forgiveness for loving things and using people rather than loving people and using things, forgiveness for procrastination in regard to a major decision, forgiveness for starting an argument rather than solving a problem, forgiveness for personal preoccupations that dull any sensitivity to others, forgiveness for inattention to your holy will.

We also pray for others—specific others: for the families of those people who died in a recent accident, for the parents of children whose deaths make no sense, for that nameless homeless man sleeping on the park bench, for that high school student who is trying to be true to her moral convictions and also achieve popularity, for persons who will not have enough food for today, for that older individual so lonely as to believe that no one any longer cares about her, for that middle-aged man who is struggling to become a person of faith.

We do want your leadership, God. Release the grip of tradition on us that we might be open to innovation. Prod us to think about the priorities of faith. Strengthen us as we make ourselves vulnerable in order that we may trust and love those most important to us.

O God, praying in specifics is taxing, a bit unnerving, and certainly self-revealing. We feel like running. But there are promises, needs, ice cream, and commitments. We simply must speak to you about these specifics. This is a beginning. Send your Spirit to sustain us that there may be no ending; in the name of the incarnate Lord. Amen.

Spring

God of all days and seasons:

Spring is here! Clearly, spring is a gift that comes straight from the heart of your creativity and love. Thank you.

Greening grass, flowering plants, and leafing trees remind us of your continuing presence in our world. New colors that explode before our eyes point us to the beauty and majesty of your Being.

Spring arrives with a special set of concerns, though. Our thanks for spring are accompanied by intercessions prompted by these concerns:

Springtime weather is often turbulent. Tornadic winds stir
up destructive forces. We pray for people who get hurt by
nature's violence. Prevent these people from feeling singled
out or punished. Enable them to find an inner peace that
remains stable regardless of howling storms and rushing
waters.

Transitions pervade the season of spring. Graduations.
Relocation. God, you know the pain of saying farewells
and moving to new communities. To all who are caught up
in transition this spring, grant a sense of confidence and
security that will relieve their anxieties and uncertainties.
Prevent any graduate from assuming that the necessity for
education has ended.

Crops are planted in the spring. O God, some of the seeds
being sown right now can mean the difference between life
and starvation for some people in the world next year. Push
those seeds into the soil to the depth they need, moisturize
and fertilize them, that in due time these seeds may bring
forth food that can be harvested and placed in the trembling
hands of hungry people.

God, we pray for the concerns of this new spring even as we give
you thanks for its riotous emergence. We rejoice that spring has come
to our world once more.

Now, God, send springtime into our lives—the newness, freshness, growth, and beauty.

Send new meaning into our lives as they begin anew. Fill us with
the power of the resurrected Lord, who is Lord of spring and summer, autumn and winter. Amen.

Stewardship

Dear God for whom sacrifice is both a gift and a request:

We realize that by making us recipients of your bountiful and
good gifts, you have made us stewards. That identity and the responsibility inherent in it cannot be denied. Our only choice is between
handling irresponsibly that which you graciously have entrusted to us
or serving as good stewards.

Clarify our vision of the scope of responsible stewardship.
Sensitize us to the truth that the greatest challenges to our stewardship coincide with our best blessings. What we have received, we are
to give.

You give us life. We must offer commitment.

You give us Scripture. We must study.

You give us music. We must make ourselves instruments of
praise.

You give us children. We must serve as good parents.
You give us talents. We must minister accordingly.
You give us church. We must extend fellowship.
You give us the gospel. We must share the Good News.
You give us each other. We must live in love.

O Giver of all that we call good and perfect, transform our gratitude for what you have placed within our hands into significant means of serving others as well as you.

We rejoice in our freedom; grant us diligence in freeing others.

We are thankful for our finances; direct our monetary
investments toward the furtherance of a gospel witness in
words and deeds.

We are grateful to be able to speak; help us to fill our words with
encouragement, instruction, and invitations to discipleship.

We are pleased to be able to act; strengthen our work on
the foundations of personal and social good will.

All of life belongs to you. We know that. And we are so very appreciative of you sharing life with us. The possibility of cooperating with you in the ongoing work of creation and redemption comes as both a blessing and a responsibility. We would not take anything for it, but we certainly need your help in order to do our best with it. Please assist us, God.

We are blessed with love. We seek to bless others with love.

We know forgiveness. We want to be forgiving.

We experience peace. We offer ourselves as peacemakers.

We are filled with the joy of redemption. We want to share
this joy by living redemptively.

Captivate our commitment to responsible stewardship, O God, and motivate us by it, so that in every area of life, we display the lordship of Christ in our lives and reveal our love for you.

In the name of the Perfect Steward we pray. Amen.

Storms

O God, Lord of creation, Sovereign of the universe:
Sometimes the nature of our lives is akin to activities in the natural realm.
Pleasant calm is threatened by warning sounds of thunder.
Peaceful darkness is cracked by sudden flashes of lightning.
Gentle breezes suddenly swell into sweeping, frightening
winds.
Just when everything seems all right, everything seems to go
wrong—
an unexpected hospitalization,
a goal unmet,
an untimely death,
disrupting change,
loss of employment,
shattered dreams,
a mandate to move,
serious surgery,
a failed test,
hurtful homesickness,
a rejected request,
a ruptured relationship.
O God of sweeping winds and gentle breezes, Lord of silence and thunder, sender of sunshine and rain:
Help us to find you amid the turbulence of our lives even as within the moments and places of peace. Enable us to sense your presence in the storm, to hear your voice in and above the thunder, to know your calm even as lightning flashes. Keep before us the truth that sunrises will come again, casting beauty while conveying warmth and joy.
We pray in the name of the One who stilled a storm on the lake and brought calm to people's lives. Amen.

Summer Heat

God of sunshine and rain, heat waves and blizzards:

It's hot! Not unusually hot, but uncomfortably hot. Though hot weather is no more than a physical, climatological fact, it does exert influence on our spirits. When the air around us is filled with heat, we often find ourselves ready to explode.

Tolerance levels are as low as anxieties are high. Anger is on edge. Tempers flare. We feel hassled, uneasy, worried. Matters otherwise easily negotiable plague us as major problems. Coping becomes difficult. Sweat on our foreheads is complemented by weariness in our souls.

God, it's hot!

God of all conditions, help us through this heat.

Prevent us from using high temperatures as an excuse for
    forfeiting responsibilities.

Encourage us to go on doing ministry even when we don't
    want to get out of our houses.

Keep our minds sharp, our consciences clear, and our
    sensitivites alert in the midst of heat that threatens to make
us dull.

Cooling is wonderful, God, even artificial cooling. As we sit in front of cool blasts from an air conditioner, though, we realize that not everyone afflicted by the summer heat has access to such luxury. Make us ministers of comfort to those devoid of help when hurt by heat.

Of course, we know full well that lasting calmness, peace, serenity, and joy come not from heat or cool air, naturally provided or artificially produced, but only by way of your merciful love. So we reach out for your mercy and love, wanting to enjoy your faithfulness.

Heat remains a concern. But not a big one. Not a major concern unless we have no promise of relief. If that is the case for anyone, touch that person with coolness even as with your loving faithfulness.

We pray in the name of One who in his vulnerability was exposed to the heat of a blistering Middle Eastern sun and who offered up his life that we might know salvation in all the seasons of our lives. Amen.

Surprise

God of the burning but unconsumed bush in the desert, daily manna
in the wilderness, and an opportunity for salvation for the world by
way of a crucifixion in Jerusalem:

God, how we love surprises!

Sometimes we think your pseudonym must be "Surprise." Who
else ever would have thought of

calling a reticent, stammering herdsman to be a mighty
prophet of liberation;

providing a fire by night and a pillar of cloud by day
for the guidance of wanderers in the wilderness;

laying hold of the on-again-off-again obedient Hebrews
as a special people of mission;

choosing a little-known village on the back side of
nowhere as the site of the most important birth in all of history;

responding to evil with good, meeting hatred with love,
and praying for enemies;

allowing people to witness on a Sunday morning the
resurrection of their beloved leader who had died and was
buried the previous Friday afternoon;

designating a fickle, fearful group of disciples as the
nucleus of a fellowship charged with the task of taking the
gospel to the whole world;

enlisting as the most influential person in the primitive
community of faith a man whose life had been devoted to
killing persons because of their affirmations of faith?

God, we love it. Life is not predictable. Change is always possible.
You do no trade with boredom.

We are confident about all of that as we look at the past. Sometimes, though, we are not so sure when we study the present. Have
surprises gone the way of miracles? Or are we just not seeing what
you are doing?

Teach us more about surprises, O God. We want to believe, need
to believe, that situations are never unchangeable, that life always
contains hope. More specifically, we need to know that

one major disappointment does not portend the destruction of
all dreams;

diversity does not negate the development of unity;

ruptured relationships can be restored;

despicable sins can be forgiven;
grief can be followed by peace and happiness;
doubt can lead to faith.

Save us from cynicism, God. Disturb us when we tend to become smug in pessimism. Create within us a holy expectation.

In other words, help us to learn how to live every day on the tiptoes of authentic faith so that we will be sensitive to the powerful rustling of your Spirit in the world, changing situations for the better or the best. We want to know the joy of seeing unexpected good and suddenly thinking to ourselves, if not saying to others, "Surprise. God has done it again."

We pray in the name of the One who turned the world and all its values upside down. Amen.

Thanks

God of grace and all other goodness:

Most of the time I feel much more deeply than I let anyone know. I'm not at all proud of that, but it's true. I find myself holding back emotions, not saying all that I want to say, even in relation to you. The time has come for that to change, and I welcome your help in making that change possible.

Thinking about reasons for giving thanks to you prompted that confession. I'm thankful for the same things everybody else is thankful for, God. You know—for family and friends, freedom and rights, food, clothing, and shelter. I have said all of those things before, countless times in routine ways. But I have a real need to say more.

I am thankful to you—profoundly grateful to you, O God—for gifts that I seldom, if ever, mention. I don't want to seem trite. I don't want to ask for your time and attention to voice inconsequential concerns. Yet I do want you to know how I really feel about the many expressions of your goodness. So here goes a different kind of prayer.

O God, I give you thanks
for wind gusts that stir swirling flurries of gold and
red autumn leaves;
for cabins without telephones and clocks;
for a child who, unintimidated by the formality of a religious

service, blurts out, "Why are we doing all of these strange things?"

for a sudden rainstorm that drenches the earth with water and fills the sky with loud rolls of thunder and brilliant zigzagging bolts of lightning;

for the sight of a sea gull gracefully gliding just before darting down into the water to snare its dinner and the haunting sound of its scream, which for a split second prevails over the noise of the rushing surf and the diversions within my heart;

for caramel-covered apples rolled in nuts and eaten off a stick;

for a teacher as devoted to students as to knowledge;

for friends whom I think of as family members;

for a heavy snow that closes down everything—even the meetings at the church;

for a first grader whose broad grin of accomplishment is completely covered with the moist pink residue of well-chewed bubble gum that exploded while inflated;

for spires atop sanctuaries that seem to represent far more than an architect's creativity;

for mud puddles to step in or around;

for a rainbow mystically arched over a meadow coming alive with the green grass and wildflowers of spring;

for lightning bugs around me and glittering stars above me on a peaceful summer night;

for an aged man whose wrinkled face bears an expression that is an irrefutable affirmation of the pleasure that is possible at every stage of life;

for the deep, resounding gongs of a tower clock striking at midnight;

for the ability to whistle;

for strawberries;

and for grace—the very idea of it, expressions from it, the peace and joy that accompany it.

O God, I am thankful to you for so much! Especially though, for strawberries and grace.

Thanks be to you through Jesus Christ who showed us how to live as well as to speak thankfully. Amen.

Time

O Timely and Timeless God:

We can't get our minds off time. We are always conscious of time, if not periodically enslaved to it. We are clock watchers and calendar turners. Repeatedly we ask: "What time is it?" "How much time will that take?" "Do we have time to finish what we have started?"

Frankly, God, a part of our difficulty in comprehending your nature stems from you being beyond time as well as in it. We are absolutely amazed that One liberated from time would choose to become involved in time—in Bethlehem, in Atlanta, in Jesus, with us. In fact, your decision and action speak volumes to us about your love and fill us with a belief that you can help us.

O God, hear our prayer about time. Forgive our sins related to time. Redeem us that we may redeem the time as you instructed.

We do not request more time or less time, for who knows what that means? Rather, we request a relationship for all times—a relationship with you. Out of your grace, fill our lives with your presence that life may be meaningful within time as we measure it and beyond time as you provide it.

We pray in the name of the Alpha and the Omega. Amen.

Transcendence

Almighty God, Ground of all being:

Surely, there is more to life than we can see, feel, and hear right now. We need a sense of transcendence. We long to hear a word from beyond us, to experience One who is greater than we are.

We are uneasy with a public so fickle in its politics that show dominates substance, pollsters direct voters, and international responsibility is made subservient to an isolationist passion for individual security.

We may need to be saved from ourselves, O God.

We are troubled by tragedies. We try to make sense of senseless accidents. We ask unanswerable questions. We judge faith by reason. We seek a hope rooted in self-potential rather than divine promise. We are in trouble as well as troubled, God. We have overextended ourselves.

Promises pile up around us.

Assignments besiege us.

Meetings demand incredible amounts of time.

Life is closing in on us.

We see no hope for ourselves apart from the salvation that comes from beyond ourselves. Divine salvation.

We request a sense of transcendence, all the while hoping that the One we discover beyond us will also come to us in love.

Is that too much to expect, God? Or is that precisely the expectation that makes us receptive to the Christ and the gospel about him?

We pray looking beyond ourselves to the transcendent-immanent Lord. Amen.

Travel

God of the wilderness wanderers and all subsequent pilgrims of faith:
Ever since we were children, most of us have liked "to go"—

to visit family members in another community,

to enjoy an amusement park in a nearby city,

to sun on the beaches of a coastal state,

to sightsee in a different part of the world.

We are very thankful for these opportunities. We do not take mobility for granted.

Frequently travel has been a teacher for us. We are grateful to you, O God, for the lessons that we have learned as a result of traveling—

that beauty has no boundaries,

that an ability to communicate is essential,

that freedom must be prized and protected,

that culture is a dominant determinant of lifestyles,

that both good and bad reside in all people.

We pray that we are not finished with traveling. We know that we are not through learning. God, please continue to use the experiences of our various expeditions to feed a permanent wisdom.

What is usually recreational for us is almost always vocational for others. We pray for those people—

for drivers, engineers, and pilots entrusted with the
safety of their passengers;

for road-weary salespersons required to be away from their
homes Monday through Friday;

for specialists and consultants who must always go whenever

and wherever their services are needed.

The next time we are on our way back from somewhere—sailing past the Statue of Liberty or flying across the Golden Gate Bridge, driving over the county line, cycling across the city limits, or rounding the corner while walking through our neighborhood—reinforce once more those wonderful realizations—

that we have a home,

that the best part of traveling is arriving back at home,

that here and there—everywhere—you are with us always.

Even if we could, we would not ever want to travel one step without you or away from you. Thank you for making that an impossibility.

We want to know your constant presence in the future with even greater intensity than we have sensed your accompaniment in the past. Since such an awareness is more up to us than to you, we promise to work on it even as we continue to pray for it.

We pray in the name of Jesus who promised us your eternal presence. Amen.

Ultimate

Everlasting God, Essence of life:

We constantly chatter with one another about what is ultimate with far more boldness and self-assurance than our competency on the subject allows. You know the rhetoric of our self-styled dreams of what is most important—

climbing to the top of the social ladder by blithely
skipping several rungs at a time;

achieving the recognition of success (not just success,
but the recognition of it) by our peers in the
professional community;

earning a salary commensurate with the costs of the
accouterments to be expected by people of status.

We know all too well the matters we treat as ultimates—

gaining membership in a certain club or organization;

making it through the year without missing a single day of
work;

positively impressing our friends while adequately arousing
envy in our enemies;

getting a meal on the household table three times a day;
receiving high marks from our superiors, be they
teachers, bosses, coaches, or elected officials.

Yes, you know and we know. But why does none of that bring us any immediate ease? How is it that what we so compulsively strive to possess as an ultimate vanishes as quickly as a mist when in our grasp? Why must we constantly be reassigning our assumptions about ultimate values?

Of course, we know that Jesus instructed us to seek first the kingdom of God and taught us to pray for your kingdom to come and for your will to be done, implying a direct relationship between those two. Candidly, though, we thought that was just church talk, fine for a Sunday school class conversation but a bit weak for most of the activities of our weeks. We missed seeing the significance of his words for our ultimate concerns. Forgive us, please, understanding God. And grant us wisdom.

More than that, stop us in our tracks every time we start to assign ultimate values to penultimate issues, and at that very moment enable us to refocus our thoughts on you and to strengthen our relational commitment to you. Imprint indelibly in our minds that only your kingdom is forever.

We pray in the name of the One who opens the eternal ultimate to us amid the temporal events of every passing day. Amen.

Vision

God of revelation and inspiration:

From your Holy Word come instructions about the necessity of vision and statements of encouragement for the entertainment of visions. Help us, O God.

We tend to harbor in our minds most readily visions of ourselves enjoying personal popularity, professional superiority, social success, and economic affluence. But we sense the ultimate meaninglessness of all that. So we turn to you in prayer with a request for visions that you have authored.

Our world needs a new vision of your sovereignty. We need negotiations more than confrontations, cooperation more than conflict, peace rather than war.

Help us, Lord!

Our world needs a new vision of your freedom. We need

    no political hostages—free them, Lord,

    no slaves of prejudice—free them, Lord,

    no bond servants to poverty—free them, Lord,

    no captives of hunger—free them, Lord,

    no servants of sin—free them, Lord.

Our world needs a new vision of your redemption. Save us, Lord. Save all of us. Enable us to call on your name in repentance, to open our hearts to you in commitment, and to bow our knees to you in obedience. You are God and there is no other!

We pray for visions that lift us out of endless despair and fill us with a hope that nurtures life-enhancing beliefs and behavior. We long to see your kingdom come and your will be done.

Our prayer is offered in the name of the One who gives clear visibility to spiritual reality. Amen.

War

God whose aggression is born of love and whose aim is peace:

War *is* hell. Channel the unwavering intensity with which we seek to avoid hell into perpetual efforts to avoid war as well; for the good of all people and the glory of Christ. Amen.

Witness

O God who never leaves a generation without a witness:

"Witness" is a word that precipitates profoundly ambivalent feelings within me. For some reason, as soon as I hear the word spoken, I feel guilt. I think I'm not doing enough. Though I am never sure I know exactly what I am "not doing enough" of, the sound of the word "witness" gives me the sense that a long, bony finger of condemnation is being pointed toward my face.

Then, too, multiple images come to mind—negative images mostly:

Memorizing a series of Bible verses along with appropriate comments to accompany them and then mechanically reciting the whole package as a "witness" applicable to anybody, anywhere, anytime.

Buttonholing a stranger and with no sense of personal compassion, not even so much as bothering to find out his name, seeking to "witness" to him—a kind of soul-oriented, spiritual counterpart to a bounty-motivated headhunter.

Individuals talking about the gospel in generalities, all of them piling one religious cliché on top of another, none of them providing any insight into their own unique pilgrimage of faith, and then dubbing such talk as a "testimony" about redemption—a festival of "witness."

I have seen so many misunderstandings, abuses, and confusions related to Christian witness that I have trouble praying about it.

However, I know, O God, that even as you have called us to be disciples of Christ, you have commissioned us to share your word, to bear witness to your grace, love, and salvation. So please hear my prayer about witness.

Bless the witness of my words. Give me the wisdom to know when to speak, to whom, and how.

Enhance the witness of my actions. Enable me somehow to live in such a manner that others will see in me a quality of life that they desire enough to ask about and pursue.

Strengthen the witness of my mind. Sustain me as I seek by both demeanor and declaration to display an unwavering devotion to truth and a lack of fear regarding old questions and new insights so that others may come to know Christ as truth.

Despite all of my weaknesses, flaws, and sins, make my life transparent to the glory of Christ's life. How you can do that is a mystery. That you can do it is a certainty. And I am more than willing to help.

This prayer is offered in the name of the One about whom enough can never be said. Amen.

Women

God of all persons, women and men, families and nations:

We speak to you concerning women—women and the church, women in the church.

Right off, help us discover from Scripture rather than from culture the meaning of being feminine. Teach us the implications of the revealed truth that both women and men are created in your image.

Stir our imaginations as we pursue the present ramifications of the persistent fidelity of women to our Lord—

traveling with him,

staying at his side through the most critical moments of
his suffering,

remaining on Golgotha until he breathed his last breath
on the cross,

approaching the place of his interment that they might
care for his body in death as they had provided for him
in life,

rushing from the empty tomb with the history-altering,
salvation-assuring news that Christ was risen.

We are moved to thanksgiving, O God, for women of faith in both the past and the present. We are mindful of how your Word has been studied and proclaimed, your ministry embraced and expressed, your church loved and strengthened by female disciples.

Personally, many of us learned our first prayers, received our earliest instructions in faith, and discovered your will through the love of a woman—a mother, a sister, a grandmother, an aunt, a wife, a neighbor, a Sunday school teacher. How much poorer would be your kingdom were it not for women. We thank you for them.

Frankly, God, these expressions of thankfulness precipitate an uneasiness fed by guilt and a confession that reaches out for forgiveness.

Forgive us for those occasions when we have treated women
as second-class citizens.
Forgive us for words, thoughts, and actions that have
reduced women to sex objects rather than wholistic persons
of dignity.
Forgive us for using gender as a justification for inequality.
Forgive us within the church for encouraging women to be
sensitive to your leadership and then slamming doors shut
in their faces—doors that lead to avenues along which their
faithful obedience can become meaningful service.
Forgive us, O God.

Now, Creator-Redeemer, lead us. Allow those of us who are men
to learn from the women around us the special traits of character that
seem dominant among females but that are needed in all persons.
Nurture us in laughter and tears together. Prevent us from excluding
women from any involvements in the church to which you have
called them. Guide us as we reflect on the revelation recorded by
Paul that in Christ there is neither male nor female.

We pray in the name of the One who affirmed the worth of
women, freed women from social stereotypes, and commissioned
women to spiritual service. Amen.

Words

O God, Source of the *dabar,* the *logos,* the Word who became flesh:
Words. Words. Words. We are surrounded by them, bombarded
by them, enticed by them, confused by them. Our ears and intellects
seem incapable of discretion. Thus, news of a crisis in the Middle
East elicits from us little more interest than advertisements for a new
toothpaste. And *the* Word, your inspired revelation, goes begging.

Most Holy One, help us to hear with sensitivity that we might
know the difference between the script of the nightly news and a text
from Genesis or Ephesians. Amid a cacophony of human sounds,
enable us to discern a holy word in order that we might hear

the good news of redemption,

the parameters of judgment,

the summons to peace,

the appeal for justice,

the message of mercy.

We seek now to still the rumblings within our souls and to focus
our attention exclusively on the biddings of your Spirit. Speak to us
just now, revealing God.

We ask in the name of the Word—the Word made Flesh. Amen.

Work

God of work and rest, the work of creation and the sabbath rest:
As we speak to you about work, we pray that we will learn and
grow as a result of your work. In creation and redemption you have
modeled the kind of meaning we must discover in all our labor.

That is really, really tough, God. So many of us are bored to tears
by what we do and even oppressed by job expectations and responsibilities devoid of significant meaning—

an assembly-line assignment that assaults personal
dignity by transforming individuals into machines
programmed only for mass production;

a secretary who has been made to feel that she is only
an answering mechanism for the telephone and a word
processor whose worth is calculated by speed;

a janitor or a maid who is forever cleaning up the
messes of others and caring for the kind of possessions

that he or she will never own.

Then, too, many of us are discouraged by the results of our work—

an athletic coach whose teams cannot ever find a way to win;

a teacher whose students show few signs of improvement
in discipline or comprehension;

an officer of the law whose fascination with community
has become buried under a preoccupation with fighting
criminality;

a counselor who watches clients disdain advice and
become mired in despair;

a houseparent whose jobs for today will be the same as
those for the next day, all devoid of any gratitude or
affirmation.

Please keep before us, O God, the worth of work—a worth
determined not by remuneration, not by quantitative production, not
by position or job description, but by personal fulfillment, spiritual
significance, and social relevance. And do not let us forget the
primacy of people. We do not practice medicine and law but help
people. We do not sell merchandise, stocks, and bonds, but help
people. We do not run an office or a company, but help people. We
do not teach school, but help people.

God, instill within us a proper understanding of the nature and
value of work—not as elaborated in *Forbes, Business Weekly,* and
The Wall Street Journal, but as revealed in Scripture. Encourage us in
that labor unconcerned about the color of our collar and not con-
sumed by passion for another dollar. Call us to and strengthen us in
work—physical or mental—which we can do with pleasure and offer
to you as worship, work by which we can witness to the world about
the importance of service to others.

We pray in the name of the carpenter from Nazareth whose
ministry began behind a work bench. Amen.

Worship (Corporate Experience)

Holy God:

We rush to worship you today. Our motivations differ, but we share a sense of urgency about this act.

Worship is a sigh for some of us. This moment is the first time in several days we have slowed down, focused upon ourselves, assessed our needs, breathed a prayer, and sought peace. We are grateful for this quiet experience in our hectic lives.

Worship is a burst of energy for others of us. This moment is the first time in several days we have had a reason to be active, to focus on others, to match talents with needs, to seek fellowship. We are grateful for this dynamic experience in our quiet lives.

We worship you, O God, with
>
> praise pulsating in our hearts,
> praise reverberating in our minds,
> praise soaring through our spirits,
> praise leaping from our lips.

Your greatness, mercy, power, grace, and love prompt our praise.

We worship you, O God, with
>
> confessions of our sins,
> requests for forgiveness,
> admissions of our weaknesses,
> pleas for strength.

Your promises, grace, and invitation prompt our confessions and requests.

We worship you, O God, with
>
> offerings,
> love, hoping to love you more profoundly,
> knowledge, longing to know you more intimately,
> actions, resolving to serve you more meaningfully.

Your goodness, gifts, and love prompt our offerings.

We worship you, O God, with commitment. Here are our lives. We commit ourselves to you.

Your commitment to us and gift of redemption for us prompt our commitment to you.

We come running to you, God, to worship you. Please accept our praise, hear our confessions, grant us pardon for our sins and strength with which to face future temptations, receive our offerings, and embrace our commitments. As we run into your presence, remind us that you lovingly and willingly run with us.

Great God! We worship you. Amen.

Worship (Personal Reactions)

O God worthy of worship:

This morning (Sunday) shortly before eleven o'clock I went to worship. I visited a church that meets in a building not far from where I live. I hate to say this, God, but it was not a good experience for me.

I really liked the way the hour began. The organ music was magnificent. Every chord seemed to move me closer to holy ground. My spirit was soaring higher and higher as the beautiful sounds from the organ grew louder and more intense. Then, right at the crescendo of the musical composition, a man seated behind me not too quietly or kindly said to his wife, "That organist always plays too loud." I could have shot him.

Several different people spoke from behind the pulpit. One young lady read a psalm that was particularly meaningful. An older man offered a prayer that gave no evidence of any forethought or purpose.

Actually, although I did not count the minutes in each segment of the service, much more time was spent talking about the various activities in which the church's members could be involved during the coming week than offering praise, encouraging faith, or even reflecting on the Bible readings. At one point, I found myself thinking that the minister showed more excitement announcing a cake-baking contest sponsored by a men's group in the church than he did repeating an assurance of the divine pardon promised to the people present who were wrestling with guilt and requesting forgiveness for their sins.

According to the printed order of worship, the sermon for the morning was based on the Gospel. If I had not read that, I would not have known it. I did not hear any good news at all. The preacher for the hour seemed mad at everybody and everything. He only smiled once or twice and then when making references to himself.

I know I am complaining a lot, God. I'm sorry! However, I really wanted to be a part of a worshiping congregation this morning. It didn't happen. Of course, by no stretch of the imagination was that your fault. Probably, you are just as disappointed about most of that hour as I am.

God, I can worship you by myself. I often do. But there is no substitute for joining with other people in adoration, praise, and thanksgiving directed to you. When confessions, offerings, and commitments to you grow out of my involvement with a fellowship, something happens that is not present when I am alone. So next Sunday I will try again. Please nudge me if I need it.

I realize that the problem this morning could have been because of something peculiar to me. Even if not, forgive me for spending so much time thinking about what was or was not going on around me and so little time concentrating on you. If I am ever in such a situation again, God, please help me to be so focused on my responsibilities in worship that I do not allow anyone else to distract me or to divert my efforts as I make the offerings and claim the promises inherent in public worship.

I pray in the name of the One whose entire life constituted an act of worship. Amen.

X-Mas

God of the Incarnation:

Surely you must laugh at our constant search for shortcuts accompanied by pseudo-sophisticated rationalizations of them. Or maybe you cry. We have a penchant for brevity and simplicity. Whatever we must do, we try to do quickly. Our favorite statements of opinions, beliefs, and convictions are those that can fit on a bumper sticker.

Somewhere, sometime, somebody started writing X-mas instead of Christmas. One letter was employed to replace six others—obviously a timesaver when you consider how many times we use the word "Christmas" during December. Then came loud protests: "Put Christ back into Christmas."

O God, who do we think we are? What audacity! Who among us can take out of history the One whom you placed there? Replacing letters in a word is one thing, but removing the reality of the Incarnation is quite another.

Predictably, attempts have been made to justify what has become common practice. Thus, some religionists have given approval to the term "X-mas" explaining that the X is a symbol for the Greek letter *chi,* which was often used as a symbol for the Christ. Great Goodness! In the time required for all the explanations of our brevity, we could have written "Christmas" repeatedly.

Honestly, God, we know the issue is not a word. Spare us from such a passion for brevity and simplicity that we imagine easy explanations for mystery, clichés about love that become more important than love, and shortcuts to salvation. Deliver us from every attempt to say and do less about your work than should be said and done. Guide us away from every effort to replace the perfect statement of your patient grace with a hurriedly scratched-out word or carried-out action that is at best an abbreviation of human concoction for the purpose of convenience.

Come to us in your fullness, O God. As you sent your Son to be born in Bethlehem, holy and wholly, send him once more to be born and to live in us.

We pray in the name of the Christ without whom there is no Christmas. Amen.

X-Rated

Creating and Redeeming God:
Sometimes life is very disturbing.

The Bible tells us that when you finished the work of creation, you surveyed what had been done and called it good. You spoke of maleness and femaleness affirmatively, causing us to understand sexuality as an integral part of your primal intentions for persons. The Scriptures also speak of the significance of the human body, describing it as a temple. You placed within people the potential for meaningful communication with one another—thoughts to share, words to speak, feelings to convey.

O God, what has happened? What on earth has happened? Why are we now confronted with books, magazines, records, tapes, pictures, and films that present people, language, and ideas under the label "x-rated"? How have individuals formed in your image reduced certain aspects of creation to a level considered off-limits to decent people?

Only now are we beginning to realize the full extent of what has been done—

the desecration of persons,
the devastation of sexuality,

the idolatry of violence,
the general pervasiveness of immoral perversions.
We are staggered by our society's capacity for corruption.

God, please forgive us. Forgive us for transforming into repugnant forms of evil that which you intended for good—

for public displays of interpersonal actions intended
for privacy alone,

for graphic depictions of intimate relations between a
variety of persons that make a mockery of your divine
plan for permanent, one-flesh unions,

for fanciful presentations of violence that confuse what
is gory with some aspects of human glory,

for market-oriented literature that perpetrates the
confusion of appropriate expressions of a covenant love
with uncontrolled, repulsive attempts at physical
gratification,

for stories that sensationalize sex by making a deity of
anatomy,

for statements that prostitute the good purposes of
language with offensive words chosen to exalt vulgarity.

O God, forgive us. Help us to restore every aspect of creation to conformity with your divine intention.

If "x-rated" is a popular designation for the evil treatment of a powerful good or for a distorted presentation aimed at making people attracted to that which should be prohibited, strengthen us as we seek to strike from our society both the label and the need for it.

If "x-rated" is another term for immorality, a label for what should be banned or eliminated within society, then in addition to aiding us in the application of it to illicit sex, obscene violence, and crude language, show us the wisdom of also branding as x-rated phenomena such as war, poverty, hunger, pollution, and prejudice.

We pray in the name of the One who willed for all of creation to be committed to the will of the Creator. Amen.

Yell

Compassionate God:

Sometimes we just want to yell, really yell—

"I hurt!"

"I am in love!"

"I am angry!"

"I am sorry!"

"I am happy!"

"Help!"

Teach us that you readily understand such impulses and invite us to direct our screams to you. Reassure us of the truths that your care is as broad as life itself and no emotion exists outside your love.

Enable us to vent pent-up emotions in healthy expressions. Guide us by means of our faith that we may know the relief of release.

Hear now our prayers—mixtures of

happiness and sadness,

anxiety and hope,

anger and love,

intercession and confession.

We pray to you because you have experienced all of that before us and invited all of that from us. You have redeemed all of that within us.

We lay bare our emotions before you and request your compassionate attention to them. Please deliver us from bondage to our emotions and make us masters over them.

Yes, sometimes we just want to yell, to scream at the top of our lungs. But at other times we seek to whisper. And at still other moments, we prefer silence. However, in all times we want to direct our words—embraced silently or spoken audibly—to you. We do so now in this prayer offered in the name of the One who invited us into your presence. Amen.

Zeal

God of revelation through zealous actions:

Zeal is a behavioral characteristic that we trust as a dimension of your divine nature, but that we regard as suspect in relation to ourselves and others. We have the sentiments, the directions of your holy zeal—

> to raise prophets,
> to provide salvation,
> to instill hope,
> to bless the poor,
> to establish justice,
> to rule with love.

However, we simply are not so sure about the virtues of human zeal.

Keep us honest, O God! Set before us the truth that the intensity of our zeal is in no sense an indication of the morality of it. Frankly, some folks are so fascinated with enthusiasm for the sake of enthusiasm that they do everything with zeal. In the Bible we even read of zeal devoted to the establishment of evil. Even a man of the stature of the apostle Paul admitted that he had killed Christians with zeal.

Grant to us the gift of discretion so that we can repudiate a superficial zeal within us, avoid an acceptance of inappropriate or morally misguided zeal by us, and incorporate a healthy constructively directed zeal in us.

Send to us great zeal

> as we seek to do your will in love,
> as we seek to establish righteousness in our lives,
> as we seek to serve persons in need in our communities,
> as we seek to embody the joy of the abundant life
> > entrusted to Christian disciples.

We pray in the name of the One who never lost his zeal for the establishment of redemption by means of a ministry of suffering love. Amen.